M☉VIE NIGHTS™

FOR TEENS

FOCUS ON THE FAMILY
RESOURCES

MOVIE NIGHTS™

FOR TEENS

25 More Movies to Spark Spiritual Discussions with Your Teen

Bob Smithouser from *Plugged In*® Magazine

TYNDALE

Tyndale House Publishers, Inc.
Wheaton, Illinois

Movie Nights for Teens
Copyright © 2005 by Focus on the Family
All rights reserved. International copyright secured.

ISBN: 1-58997-215-5

A Focus on the Family book published by
Tyndale House Publishers, Wheaton, Illinois 60189

TYNDALE is a registered trademark of Tyndale House Publishers, Inc. Tyndale's quill
logo is a trademark of Tyndale House Publishers, Inc.

All Scripture quotations, unless otherwise indicated, are taken from the *Holy Bible,
New International Version®*. NIV®. Copyright © 1973, 1978, 1984 by International
Bible Society. Used by permission of Zondervan Publishing House. All rights reserved.

Library of Congress Cataloging-in-Publication Data
Smithouser, Bob.
  Movie nights for teens : 25 more movies to spark spiritual discussions with your
teen / Bob Smithouser.
     p. cm.
   ISBN 1-58997-215-5
  1. Motion pictures—Moral and ethical aspects. 2. Motion pictures—Religious
aspects. 3. Motion pictures and youth. I. Title.
   PN1995.5.S638 2005
   791.43'653—dc22

                                                    2005011032

Editor: Kathy Davis
Cover design: Sally Leatherman
Cover photo: Getty Images

Printed in the United States of America
1 2 3 4 5 6 7 8 9 / 10 09 08 07 06 05

Contents

Introduction

Enjoying Parent-Teen Dates with a Purpose

"Movies are the highest popular art of our time, and art has the ability to change lives."—Horror novelist Stephen King[1]

No matter how you feel about Stephen King and his macabre brand of fiction, the author makes an excellent point. The questions then become: Which movies do your teenagers watch? And what sort of change is taking place, both *in* young viewers and *through* them?

The good news is that you can shape the answers to those questions. This book will help. Designed as a complement to the original *Movie Nights, Movie Nights for Teens* features films carefully selected for their ability to lead you and your adolescent into new arenas of discussion and discovery. Since more than half of these titles have been released since 2000, the stories and stars are sure to resonate with young people. Even if they've seen the movies before, experiencing them as part of a Movie Night guarantees they'll never see them the same way again. Before we get to the movies themselves, let's take a fresh look at why it makes sense to turn Hollywood's best efforts into enjoyable parent-teen dates with a purpose.

The Persuasive Power of Film

Anyone who has ever left the cinema excited, angry, inspired, or choking back tears knows that movies aren't "just entertainment." They can touch us deeply . . . for better or for worse. How deeply? In 2003, young

1

fans rushed out to buy clown fish like the ones in *Finding Nemo*. Then, in an attempt to set their pets free, a merciful misinformed minority imitated a scene from the movie and flushed them down the toilet.[2] Earlier that year a more tragic headline told of a teenager who drowned when he and his friends tried to copy a dangerous underwater training sequence from the surfing movie *Blue Crush*.[3]

Adults take cues from the big screen too. When the Jack Nicholson film *About Schmidt* mentioned a nonprofit humanitarian group by name, child sponsorships shot up from three per day to 80 per day.[4] And immediately following the release of *Sideways,* restaurants saw a disproportionate increase in requests for the main character's wine of choice. Sommelier Rob Bigelow said, "The impact of the movie on sales is huge. It's almost as though it's introducing people to Pinot Noir."[5]

Those are just a few sobering reminders that we need to teach teens to process film through a Christian filter. The following statements from industry insiders should inspire us to double our efforts:

- "The role of the artist is manipulation. We're moving into a post-literate world." —Actor/producer Ron Silver[6]
- "When you make a film you keep people captive for two hours and if you have nothing to say, or the wrong thing to say, it can have a really negative impact." —Actress Reese Witherspoon, star of *Legally Blonde* and *Sweet Home Alabama*[7]
- "I remember as a kid seeing *Rocky*. When it was done I walked out of the theater and thought, 'Man, I want to fight someone now.' I felt that juiced up." —*Clueless* co-star Paul Rudd[8]
- "I equate movies, in a visceral kind of way, to either sex or drugs. You're getting high. Or you're being turned on." —Quentin Tarantino, director of *Kill Bill* and *Pulp Fiction*[9]

Why do movies leave that kind of mark, sometimes without our even knowing we've been branded? Because there's something inherently powerful about stories. That's why Jesus used parables to teach important lessons to His disciples.

For example, in Matthew 7:24-27 Jesus could have said, "The world is unstable. Follow me." Short and to the point. Ready to move on to the next lesson. That's probably how we tend to instruct our own children, which elicits little more than a grunt and a nod. But not the Lord. Instead, Jesus told a story about two aspiring home owners who built

2

their houses on different foundations. The wise man chose rock. The foolish man trusted in sand to support his abode. Jesus proceeded to describe a storm that buffeted both structures. One stood up to the elements. The other fell. He concluded this brief but substantial analogy by comparing Himself to the solid rock that served as the wise man's starting point. In just four sentences Christ crafted a plot, characters, conflict, and a moral to the story. It captivated His audience at an emotional level, which is what makes any message stick.

That doesn't mean we have to script a one-act play for every moral we want our teens to internalize. It should, however, encourage us to look for teachable moments in well-crafted stories—including movies. Robert K. Johnston agrees, and adds a sense of urgency. The professor of theology and culture at Fuller Theological Seminary believes using contemporary parables to explore issues of faith is critical if we don't want to lose the next generation. "Film, especially for those under 35, is the medium through which we get our primary stories, our myths, our read on reality. . . . As the culture has moved from a modern to a postmodern era, we have moved from wanting to understand truth rationally to understanding truth as it's embedded in story."[10]

CALVIN AND HOBBES © 1993 Watterson. Dist. by UNIVERSAL PRESS SYNDICATE. Reprinted with permission. All rights reserved.

Preparing Teens for the Road Ahead

Clearly, we need to help teens grow in their ability to process movies. Which ones? That's up to you. The titles in this book, while not officially endorsed by Focus on the Family, are a decent place to start. Keep in mind that every child is different. Family standards can vary, even

3

among Christians. And a few of these films probably should be reserved for older teens (as noted in the "Cautions" section of each).

One of the great challenges of parenting is striking the delicate balance between *protecting* a child from the culture and *preparing* her to evaluate and engage it from a biblical perspective. When my children were in preschool, 90 percent of my job as a screener of DVDs involved protecting. They got very used to hearing the word "no." As they matured and their cognitive skills developed, I remained a protector but found myself in "preparing mode" a bit more often. That will increase as we move into the teen years. As parents steer their children toward independence, we should control their choices less and step up the sort of interaction that will prepare them to *own* those decisions as responsible adults. That takes discernment (see Appendix III). It also takes practice. The best way to encourage good habits is to ride shotgun with them for as long as we can.

Speaking of riding shotgun, you wouldn't fork over the car keys and let your daughter drive alone on the interstate her first time behind the wheel. You start out slowly, perhaps in an empty parking lot. Once she has a feel for the vehicle and you've coached her on the basics, you venture onto a deserted back road. Then, confident she'll keep it between the lines, you try a slightly busier part of town. She develops confidence and experience with you in the passenger seat, making for a smoother transition when she's ready to go solo.

And so it is with media discernment. We know our children will someday travel through the culture alone. It's part of growing up. They'll attend movies and rent DVDs without us. Will they make their choices based on Philippians 4:8 and Psalm 101:3, or will they rely on a cool TV commercial, peer pressure, or the sales pitch printed on the back of the DVD case? That depends on the investment you make now. By discussing healthy boundaries and dissecting good films together while they're still at home, you can give them the confidence, experience, motivation, and practical tools necessary to make wise choices for life.

As you get ready to teach teens how to process and apply positive Hollywood parables, don't forget the four Ps:

Preview – It's always wise to view a film yourself before using it in a Movie Night setting. Along with the "Cautions" section, this preview will help you gauge age-appropriateness, prepare you for any questionable scenes, and give you a leg up on the discussion material.

4

Pray – Before and after the preview, ask God to be part of the process. Pray for wisdom to know if and how you should use that particular movie. The Lord knows your teen's heart better than you do. Ask Him to guide your discussion for maximum benefit.

Predict – Anticipate how the film might connect with your teenager. Be sensitive to ways specific scenes or lines of dialogue could hit close to home.

Protect – Remember that each Movie Night is an exclusive date between you and your teen. Plan ahead to limit interruptions. Turn off your cell phones. Get the rest of the family occupied elsewhere. Make it the sole activity for the evening so that neither of you is in a hurry to wrap things up in order to do something else.

FOXTROT © 1998 Bill Amend. Reprinted with permission of UNIVERSAL PRESS SYNDICATE. All rights reserved.

Help Them Develop Self-Awareness

In addition to gaining a deeper understanding of the world around them, teens taught to see beneath the surface of movies will develop a better understanding of themselves—their thoughts, their feelings, why films appeal to them as they do.

Spider-Man revived the comic book superhero genre when it swung into theaters in the summer of 2002. Informal exit polls of teens asking what they liked about the movie typically drew comments about its amazing special effects, wild action, interesting story, or how well it was adapted for the screen. Pretty superficial stuff.

Imagine a 15-year-old boy depositing his popcorn bag in a nearby trash can before announcing to the pollster, "I identified with the movie because it's essentially a fantasy about a bullied teen who's allowed to transcend his circumstances with the help of cool superpowers. Kids like

5

me aren't great athletes. The cute girls don't notice us. Deep down we all wish we could be transformed overnight. But get this: Even after being empowered, the hero still struggled with social acceptance. He proved you can climb walls, spin webs, be really strong, and *still* have issues. Dude, I can relate to that!"

It's safe to say independent research firms hired by Columbia Pictures weren't hearing much of that. Still, adolescent audiences were feeling it. They may not have been aware of it or able to articulate it, but those themes connected with them just the same. Maybe that's one reason the *Spider-Man* franchise has succeeded while most of the superhero flicks that swung into theaters on its heels failed. Young people want a hero they can identify with. We just need to help them understand the connection. The same teens who take great pride in accessing the deepest levels of a video game can, with the help of a loving parent and a cinematic parable, do the same with their own thoughts and emotions.

Armed to Engage a Postmodern World

Beyond teaching teens how to deconstruct movies and understand themselves better, Movie Nights can also inspire them to share the gospel in unique, culturally relevant ways.

In his book *Basic Christianity,* Reverend John Stott mourned, "The great tragedy in the church today is that evangelicals are biblical, but not contemporary, while liberals are contemporary, but not biblical. We need faithfulness to the ancient word and sensitivity to the modern world."[11] The apostle Paul understood that balancing act. While in Athens he addressed a council named for Ares, the Greek god of war. Without compromising the gospel, Paul used an inscription from a local pagan altar ("To an Unknown God") as a jumping-off point to tell the council about the God who *can* be known (Acts 17:16–34). Paul even quoted their poets back to them (v. 28) before calling the people to repentance and telling them about Christ's resurrection.

Teens can do the same today if they learn to deconstruct film, hold the pieces up to the light of biblical truth, and apply them in a meaningful way. All truth is God's truth, whether or not the artist acknowledges the source. Take advantage of good art. Your teen knows classmates who might never set foot inside a church but would gladly discuss a movie over Tater Tots in the high school cafeteria.

Meanwhile, being able to build a scriptural bridge to film will allow your teen to defend himself against "hollow and deceptive philosophy" (Colossians 2:8), help him resist being "conformed to the pattern of this world" (Romans 12:2), and equip him to "demolish arguments and every pretension that sets itself up against the knowledge of God, and take captive every thought to make it obedient to Christ" (2 Corinthians 10:5).

Parental Guidance

You're almost ready to launch into a Movie Night experience. But before you do, have you found yourself asking any of these questions?

I've always wondered how movies get their ratings. Who determines what label a film should receive?

The ratings are assigned by an anonymous board of 12 parents living in Southern California. This panel is selected and monitored by the Motion Picture Association of America (MPAA), which pays members an undisclosed sum for a tour of duty that averages about four years. The job is simple. They sit in a private screening room, scribble notes, and discuss what they saw. Each intuitively decides the age-appropriateness of a given film and casts a written vote for a particular rating. Majority rules. That's pretty much it.

Sometimes a producer or studio will appeal the rating. They can't talk to the board directly, but rather through an MPAA executive who explains the reason for the ruling. Then the filmmaker has the option of editing the movie to secure a less severe rating. As a result, Hollywood has learned to work the system. That usually involves trimming an R picture just enough to get it a more financially lucrative PG-13. One criticism of the ratings board is that, because it doesn't have concrete criteria for assigning specific labels, filmmakers rely heavily on precedent and are finding new ways to get away with edgy content. The ratings G, PG, PG-13, and R give families a helpful starting point, but it's hard to trust a system proven to be subjective, arbitrary, and full of loopholes.[12] Film critic Steven Greydanus warns, "Parents shouldn't count on the MPAA system to do their job for them. No matter what the rating is, parental guidance is *always* required."[13]

So, how was this imperfect system born? After abolishing the conservative Hays Production Code (deemed too restrictive for the social evolution

7

of the mid-1960s), MPAA President Jack Valenti replaced it with the modern ratings system. It has evolved since 1968 but its purpose remains the same: Even more than a tool to inform parents, it is Hollywood's attempt to regulate itself, giving filmmakers artistic freedom while avoiding government censorship. Perhaps we shouldn't be surprised. The MPAA has always been the industry's lobbying arm, made up of the seven major Hollywood studios and the National Association of Theater Owners.

To learn more about the priorities and inner workings of the MPAA, starting with its ratings system, visit mpaa.org/movieratings/about/content.htm#1. If you want more detailed information about the content of specific films (what those ratings *don't* tell you), go to Focus on the Family's entertainment review site, pluggedinonline.com.

Are there general questions I could ask that would apply to any movie?

Absolutely. In addition to the ones featured in the "Talking Points" section of each Movie Night, you can refer back to this list at any time:

- Which character did you admire most? Why?
- Do the themes in this movie reflect reality? Do they reflect *truth*?
- How do the morals onscreen compare with the values you've been taught at home, in school, or in church?
- Do you think movies like this have any effect on how close you feel to your family, friends, or God? Explain.
- How might you imagine God reacting to this movie? Why? Would you feel comfortable if Jesus sat here watching it with you? (See Matthew 28:20.)
- In addition to God's opinion of the movie, does the movie have an opinion of God? What is it?
- What would happen if you imitated the lifestyles or choices of the characters? Do consequences reflect those in the real world?
- What would you say is the main point of this movie? Do you agree or disagree with it?

My daughter is 10. How young is too young to start using movies as a teaching tool?

That depends on the movie. A handful of the titles in this book, such as *My Dog Skip*, *Spellbound*, and *The Incredibles*, might be perfect for you right now. Your family may want to wait a few years and "grow into" others. Furthermore, there may be some you never feel completely comfortable with. That's fine, too. Families are different, and not all films will be a good fit in every home. The important thing is to find age-appropriate movies and start children developing critical thinking skills as soon as possible.

How young is too young? I remember watching Disney's *Beauty and the Beast* with my three-year-old daughter. If you've seen that film you may recall the first big musical number. Villagers exchange opinions of Belle while the sweet girl strolls through the streets, imagining a world beyond her provincial town. Gaston, a conceited lout, tells his sidekick he plans to marry Belle because she's "the most beautiful girl in town. That makes her the best." I hit pause. My little girl was not about to grow up thinking that physical beauty is the measuring stick by which women should be measured. Rather than ripping the tape out of the VCR, I made eye contact with her and calmly said, "Sweetie, Gaston is wrong. Belle is the best because she has a good heart. Being pretty is just a bonus." I gave her a kiss and got a smile in return. Not sure how deeply it would sink in, I pressed play and we enjoyed the rest of the movie.

I'm happy to report that it did sink in. We also owned the soundtrack. Consequently, that same song commonly played during tea parties and puzzle time. Over the next few years, every time the line came on, Shelby would look up from whatever she was doing and say quietly, "No, Daddy, it's her *heart*," grinning as though we shared a precious secret.

My children are older now, but still not mature enough for the films featured in *Movie Nights for Teens.* Until they are, we're enjoying the ones highlighted in *Movie Nights for Kids,* which could give you a good head start as well.

• • •

Finally, Movie Nights are intended to be enjoyable dates for you and your teen—the key word being *enjoyable.* Yes, we want to teach teens to look beneath the surface at what movies are really saying. Yes, we want to extract positive values from films and apply them to our lives. Yes, we want to help young people understand the concept of biblical discernment and establish healthy criteria for renting videos. And yes, we even want to figure out ways to use movies to share eternal truths with the world around us. But the primary goal is for you and your teen to share a good time together. Pop the popcorn, ice the drinks, and have fun at the movies!

THE MOVIES

Anna and the King

Rated: PG-13
Themes: Courage, slavery, respecting authority, appreciating diverse cultures, justice vs. grace, monogamy, betrayal, overcoming loss, friendship, differences between Christianity and Buddhism
Running Time: 2 hours, 27 minutes
Starring: Jodi Foster as Anna Leonowens; Chow Yun-Fat as King Mongkut; Tom Felton as Louis; Bai Ling as Tuptim
Directed by: Andy Tennant

Cautions

This true story contains mature themes and a few intense scenes best reserved for older teens and adults. While it doesn't promote Buddhism, the pervasiveness of Eastern religious idols and ideals warrants discussion. Dialogue alludes to the king's many wives and concubines. The film's most jarring moments, however, are violent ones. Victims of political unrest hang from trees. A man is shot in the head at close range. Others are shot during military or guerrilla attacks. A group of soldiers is poisoned. The most tense, disturbing scene involves a public beheading (avoid the worst of it by tuning out for 1:40 after Anna's Bible falls to the floor).

Story Summary

After spending most of her life in colonial India, British widow Anna Leonowens and her young son Louis head to Siam at the behest of King Mongkut to teach his eldest son English and instruct him in the ways of the West. They arrive in Bangkok in 1862

13

carrying luggage, a Bible, and an air of British superiority. Mother and son get a cool reception. It seems that, with England flexing its muscles around the world, some Siamese fear encroachment by the very empire she represents.

Meanwhile, Mongkut perpetuates a dynasties-old tradition of haughty chauvinism and imperious intimidation, and views Western education as a necessary evil. He rules a country steeped in Buddhism. He shares the royal palace with 23 wives, 42 concubines, and 58 children. Subjects fall prostrate in his presence. So how will he handle being challenged by a strong-willed Englishwoman who, despite wanting to show respect, runs roughshod over Siamese protocol and bristles at social injustice? Not well at first. In fact, Mongkut rewards Anna's effrontery with the assignment to educate his *entire* brood.

Their tempestuous start slowly gives way to mutual admiration. He's not the tyrant she first imagined him to be. And Anna models strength, intelligence, and wisdom, whether disciplining insolent children, defending an unjustly treated bondservant, or organizing a diplomatic dinner and defusing an awkward moment. During that event Mongkut honors her with a dance. It makes an impression—politically and personally. But any progress made between Anna and the king takes a devastating hit when Mongkut sends star-crossed lovers to their deaths in an attempt to save face. It seems his newest wife, Tuptim (given by her father), was so heartbroken at being torn from her true love that she snuck off to her soul mate's monastery, disguising herself as a Buddhist priest to be near him. Their public execution convinces Anna that she doesn't belong in Siam.

Lest viewers assume that *Anna and the King* is all about romance, it's not. The crux of the story involves political unrest, treachery, and a plot to destroy the royal family. Since Burma is a British protectorate, the fact that Burmese death squads have been attacking Siamese merchants and

14

villages has Mongkut and his advisors worried. Retaliation could invite war with Britain. Still, something must be done. A traitor in their midst sets a plan in motion to intentionally thrust Siam into war and unseat Mongkut from the throne.

The trap is sprung after Anna has left for the docks. The best Mongkut can hope to do is create a deception that will buy him time to hide his children. The king's servant urges Anna to return and care for the little ones. She agrees. Cornered, Mongkut rides out to confront his enemies in what he realizes could be a suicide mission to preserve the royal line. But sharp wits and a lot of gunpowder save the day. Anna's and Mongkut's deep affection for one another leads to one last dance before she departs for England. He tells her that, until now, he could never understand how "a man could be satisfied with only one woman."

In a final voice-over the grown prince recalls, "Anna had shined such a light on Siam." Indeed, Anna Leonowens's influence led Mongkut's heir to abolish slavery, reform the judicial system, and institute religious freedom. This Christian woman's assignment wasn't to evangelize a Buddhist nation. Even so, her courageous, wise, loving example gained the respect of its leaders and created openness to Christian thought.

Before You Watch

Much like Anna Leonowens, the prophet Daniel found himself—by his wisdom, spiritual integrity, and noble example—influencing a nation that didn't worship God. During your family devotional time, study snapshots from his life chronicled in Daniel 1-2 and 5:29-6:28. We may never find ourselves attempting to gain royal favor through uncompromising lifestyle evangelism, but we still must submit to teachers, bosses, and others in authority who can be inspired to see Jesus Christ differently by actions that speak louder than words.

Bible Bookmarks

Dan. 1-2, 5:29-6:28; Rom. 5:15-20, 8:16-18, 13:1; Jn. 3:16-18, 16:33; Ps. 22:24, 34:19; 2 Cor. 1:3-11; 1 Kgs. 11:1-13; Matt. 5:14-16

Talking Points

1. How do Anna's early struggles exemplify what missionaries face entering a foreign culture? Apply Romans 13:1. Can Christians armed with eternal truth project an air of arrogance and superiority, just as Anna did about being British? In what ways? What "foreign culture" could you influence right where you live? How can witnessing Anna's maturity help us to, first and foremost, love people where they are?

2. Read about Solomon's harem and idolatry in 1 Kings 11:1-13. Compare his behavior to King Mongkut's. Was one more right than the other? Discuss the challenge, when trying to reach the lost, of loving sinners without giving the impression that God approves of their lifestyle.

3. Buddhists conclude that "all life is suffering." How does the personal, loving God of the Bible want us to view suffering? Read Psalm 22:24 and 34:19, 2 Corinthians 1:3-11, Romans 8:16-18, and John 16:33. Has the Lord comforted you amid pain? How?

4. Why are slavery and other forms of oppression no big deal to a society that believes "all life is suffering"? What fundamental beliefs in America are reflected in how we treat each other?

5. What did Anna mean when she told the prince, "Most people don't see the world the way it is; they see it as *they* are"? How should Christians view the world . . . and themselves?

6. Mongkut realized that monogamy is better than a revolving door of sexual encounters with numerous partners. How does that testify to the fact that God designed sex for *intimacy,* not mere recreation? Do people still fail to grasp that truth? How? What are some consequences?

7. Louis and the prince get off to a rough start, but manage to become friends. What caused conflict early in their relationship? How do you think they overcame it? Have you ever made a friend out of an enemy? Do you need to?

8. During Anna's science experiment she warns the children not to assume that difficult tasks are impossible, noting, "One way to achieve the impossible is to change the climate." Are you dealing with a problem that seems unsolvable? Might changing the climate affect the outcome? Consider the possibilities. What can you do to get things started?

9. Why do you think the authorities dealt so severely with Tuptim's crime of passion? Contrast Mongkut's unbending desire to enforce the law and "save face" with how God demonstrated mercy and grace in redeeming us (John 3:16-18, Romans 5:15-20).

10. The grown prince recalls, "Anna had shined such a light on Siam." Read Matthew 5:14-16. Ask, "Is your lamp under a bowl or on a stand?" If you've seen your teen's light shining brightly, take this opportunity to describe what you've witnessed and how proud you are.

Follow-Up Activity

Teens unfamiliar with Buddhism might benefit from comparing its esoteric beliefs with core Christian truths. An outstanding way to do this is with the help of *The Spirit of Truth and the Spirit of Error 2: World Religions*, Steven Cory's foldout pamphlet from Moody Publishers that provides a side-by-side analysis of Christianity and other world religions, including Buddhism. Another brilliant resource (available in adult and teen versions) is the book *Jesus Among Other Gods* by renowned Christian apologist Ravi Zacharias.

If you enjoyed the epic story of Anna Leonowens and King Mongkut, consider renting the Oscar-winning 1956 musical *The King and I*, starring Yul Brynner and Deborah Kerr.

Just for Fun

Young Tom Felton is likable here as Anna's son, Louis. However, millions of moviegoers love to hate him in the recurring role he has become most famous for—Harry Potter's malicious rival, Draco Malfoy.

—*Bob Smithouser*

Ben-Hur

Rated: G
Themes: Christ's sacrifice, friendship, betrayal, perseverance, vengeance, forgiveness, pride, mercy, peace, God's grace and healing
Running Time: 3 hours, 32 minutes
Starring: Charlton Heston as Judah Ben-Hur; Stephen Boyd as Messala; Hugh Griffith as Sheik Ilderim; Jack Hawkins as Quintus Arrius; Haya Harareet as Esther
Directed by: William Wyler

Cautions

Some intense action and violence will seem harsh for a G movie, but should pose no problem for teens. There are whippings, beatings, and other cruel acts (including Christ's crucifixion) by Roman soldiers. A battle at sea features sword fighting and bloodied slaves struggling to escape a sinking galleon. Men get trampled when chariots wreck during a big race.

Story Summary

This winner of 11 Academy Awards (including 1959's Best Picture) is subtitled *A Tale of the Christ* because the title character periodically encounters an enigmatic Nazarene carpenter whose face we never see. It is a reverent tribute to Jesus, though the story focuses primarily on the trials, travels, and triumphs of Judah Ben-Hur, a Judean nobleman convicted of a crime he didn't commit by Messala, a boyhood companion who has become an ambitious, malicious Roman tribune.

19

The time is A.D. 26. Judah, his mother, and sister welcome Messala after years apart, but pleasantries turn to hostility when Judah refuses to sell out countrymen who oppose Rome's intrusive rule. A freak accident involving a parading governor and loose roof tiles gives Messala an excuse to make an example of Judah ("By condemning without hesitation an old friend I shall be feared"). The women are imprisoned. Judah's strong back makes him a valuable galley slave.

After three years of rowing Roman warships and tasting the cruel sting of a whip, Judah finds himself aboard the galleon of military consul Quintus Arrius. Their ship falls under attack. Judah saves Arrius' life, earning him the emperor's thanks and the freedom to serve as Arrius' slave. But Arrius respects him too much for that. In Rome, Judah becomes a respected member of the consul's household—not to mention an excellent charioteer—before being legally adopted as his heir. Judah accepts Arrius' signet ring, yet feels called to leave these comforts and return home.

On his way back to Jerusalem, Judah encounters a wealthy sheik with splendid Arabian horses who asks him to drive his team to victory over the undefeated champion, Messala. Although tempted by the offer, Judah's quest to free his mother and sister takes priority. So does his yearning for a less sporting form of vengeance.

Judah arrives home to find his household dark and neglected. His servant Esther is there to embrace him, and they soon express a long-unspoken love for one another. She warns him to let go of his hatred, quoting the teacher who draws crowds on the hillside. Reluctantly, Judah decides he will forgive Messala if the tribune restores his mother and sister to him. Messala, somewhat intimidated by Judah's new status, agrees to find and release them if they are still alive.

Sadly, the women have developed leprosy in prison. They appear briefly to Esther, but demand that she tell Judah they are dead, which she does. Overcome by grief and rage, Judah decides to reconsider the sheik's challenge to work with his horses and humble Messala in the arena. Judah wins, and in the process Messala's dirty play leads to his own fatal injuries. With Messala's body broken and bleeding, the proud, cold-hearted Roman takes a final stab at his old friend by telling Judah that his family can be found in the Valley of the Lepers.

What changed Messala? What destroyed Judah's family? What scourge threatens freedom? *Rome.* At least that's Judah's opinion. The bitter, tormented Judean prince respectfully returns Arrius' ring and embraces his former identity, though Esther claims she hardly recognizes the venomous man he has become. She speaks hopefully about the ideals of Jesus. Forgiveness. Love. Faith. Heaven. Then she and Judah prepare to take his mother and sister to the young rabbi, only to learn that the authorities have arrested him. A throng watches Jesus march toward Calvary. Then Judah has an encounter with Christ that changes him. And everyone learns that there is healing in the cross.

Before You Watch

Remind your teen that, unlike today's computer-enhanced blockbusters, *Ben-Hur* is an old-fashioned epic made decades before the advent of the technical wizardry we now take for granted. The extras are actors. And the stunts are real.

Bible Bookmarks

Gen. 37-45; Lk. 5:12-16, 17:11-19; Jer. 29:11-12; Jn. 4:13-14, 15:19, 17:14-19; 1 Pet. 3:15, 5:7; Rom. 8:28, 12:17-21; Matt. 6:26, 26:6; 1 Jn. 2:15-17

Talking Points

1. Much of *Ben-Hur* is its own spiritual reward—a straightforward presentation of Christian themes just asking to be explored further. Ask, "What moment was most meaningful to you?" and "How did you feel about the way Jesus came across?" Talk about the filmmakers' overall attitude toward Christianity and how that differs from most Hollywood portrayals today.

2. What does Messala mean when he tells Judah, "It's a Roman

world. If you want to live in it you must become part of it"? Can you think of a modern parallel? What do John 15:19, 17:14-19, and 1 John 2:15-17 warn Christians about becoming enmeshed in a worldly culture?

3. Sometimes childhood friends are tight because they live nearby, end up in the same class at school, or their parents are close. As they mature, however, different goals and values can drive a wedge between them. That seemed to be the case with Judah and Messala. Have you experienced this personally? With whom? What came between you?

4. Quintus Arrius is a faithless man who tells Judah, "Whoever the gods are, they take small interest in an old man's hopes." How do we know that God loves us? Do you feel that God takes an interest in the smaller aspects of your life? What evidence do you have (in addition to Jeremiah 29:11-12, 1 Peter 5:7, Matthew 6:26)?

5. Upon meeting Judah, Arrius belittles him for trusting in God and clinging to hope ("It's a strange stubborn faith you keep to believe that existence has a purpose"). What would you say if someone told you that believing in God is vain superstition and that life is pointless? Remember, silence is not an option (1 Peter 3:15).

6. Which characters show loyalty, mercy, or compassion? How? How are they rewarded?

7. Judah's thirst for vengeance meets with cooler heads in Balthazar and Esther. Read Romans 12:17-21. Have you been tempted to strike back at someone who has hurt you? Talk through that and choose to leave it in God's hands.

8. How did you feel when Jesus offered the shackled Judah a drink? What about when Judah returned the favor on the road to Calvary?

9. Put yourself in Esther's position. What would you have done when asked to lie to Judah about his mother and sister's fate? Why?

10. Judah complained to Balthazar that, in spite of having received water from Jesus, he remained thirsty. What was he *really* thirsty for? Examine Judah's similarities to the woman at the well introduced in John 4:7.

11. Before the chariot race, Judah essentially prays, "Forgive me for the sin I'm about to commit, but I'm going to do it anyway." Have you ever found yourself praying like that? About what? How do you think God feels when we know what's right but ignore it? Why do you think we're so stubborn?

12. Does seeing leprosy portrayed this way provide a deeper appreciation of Jesus' interactions with lepers? How? Revisit some of those events in Matthew 26:6, Luke 5:12-16, and 17:11-19.

13. Balthazar says of the Messiah, "He lives and all our lives from now on will carry his mark." Do you carry the mark of Jesus? If so, how has that changed you? What sort of mark do you hope to leave on others?

Follow-Up Activity

During your family devotions, read about the life of Joseph in Genesis 37-45. Note how his journey is similar to Judah Ben-Hur's: He was betrayed by a "brother." He spent years in slavery for a crime he didn't commit. He never lost faith. He did a heroic deed for an important leader. He was appointed to a position of power and authority. Discuss how this illustrates Romans 8:28, which reminds us that God will use setbacks and disappointments for our ultimate benefit if we keep our eyes on Him.

Just for Fun

When he started writing the novel in the late 1800s, General Lew Wallace was spiritually ambivalent. But a chance encounter with the vehemently agnostic Robert Ingersoll changed that . . . and ultimately changed *Ben-Hur*. Ingersoll's anti-God diatribe led Wallace to rethink his story and set out to make the case for Christ's divinity. Soon Wallace experienced a conversion much like that of his main character.

—*Brandy Bruce*

Bobby Jones: Stroke of Genius

Rated: PG
Themes: Integrity, sportsmanship, perseverance, innocent romance, money in sports, controlling temper, battling illness, repentance, respect, imitating others, handling pressure, learning from mistakes
Running Time: 2 hours, 9 minutes
Starring: Jim Caviezel as Bobby Jones; Jeremy Northam as Walter Hagen; Claire Forlani as Mary Malone; Malcolm McDowell as O. B. Keeler
Directed by: Rowdy Herrington

Cautions

This film could've included less alcohol and fewer profanities (about 40, most erupting from golfers after bad shots). The worst is "s—fire." It's troubling to hear it, especially from a young boy, but it's a rough edge in Bobby's character that gets sanded off, and it makes the point that children mimic inappropriate behavior.

Story Summary

In 1930, Robert Tyre Jones Jr. did what no golfer had ever accomplished and none has ever repeated. He won the Grand Slam. However, *Bobby Jones: Stroke of Genius* is less about that monumental achievement than the years leading up to it and how, by overcoming bad habits and developing solid character, Jones proved himself worthy of admiration. This leisurely paced true story stars

Caviezel, fresh from the title role in *The Passion of the Christ*, as the principled amateur who refused to turn pro.

Young Bobby Jones is a frail child forbidden to play baseball with the other boys. So he turns to golf and studies the technique of Stuart Maiden, a pro hired to coach his inept father who uses the links as a networking tool for his Georgia law practice. Maiden crafts a set of clubs for the lad, who gets hooked. At 14, the hyper-competitive newcomer is teeing off against men twice his age, and turning heads. Bobby attracts the attention of sportswriter O. B. Keeler who proceeds to follow the prodigy. Keeler and others are impressed with his skill but chagrined at his temper.

As an adult, Bobby makes higher education and an honorable career his top priorities. He studies to be an engineer and, eventually, a lawyer. Golf consumes him the rest of the time, though he insists on remaining an amateur. No cash prizes. No endorsement deals. Conversely, his arrogant, hard-living rival Walter Hagen tells him, "Y'know why *I* play golf? For the money. I *have* to win, which is why whenever you come up against me I'm gonna beat you." Sometimes he does. Sometimes he doesn't. Over the years "Sir" Walter resents having to share the spotlight, yet respects Bobby's integrity and decency.

Another love enters Bobby's life in Mary Malone, a sweet, modest young lady who supports his quest to fulfill everyone's high expectations of him on the golf course. He goes through a difficult stretch, at one point getting so frustrated with the conditions that he quits mid-round. Pressure keeps mounting. It doesn't help to know that his pious, industrious grandfather considers driving, chipping, and putting a colossal waste of time.

Despite being humble and gracious with everyone he meets, Bobby continues to battle what one writer calls his "smoldering wrath" on the fairways. It flares up one day during a tournament. A thrown club strikes a spectator on the leg, causing Bobby's father and golf authorities to read him the riot act. It's a turning point for the repentant athlete, as is a surprise telegram from his grandfather expressing favor and encouragement. Energized and imbued with confidence, Bobby proceeds to win the 1923 U.S. Open and go on a roll. He gets married. He turns another tassel. He starts selling real estate. A baby arrives. Even when he loses a match by one stroke, it becomes a moral victory that deepens others' respect for him. Indeed, everything's going his way.

Soon, however, Bobby's body starts to betray him. A rare neurological disorder is compounded by exhaustion. Unwilling to slow down, he relies on medicine to get by. Mary begins to resent the sport that's tearing away at her husband. He assures her that, after he takes a crack at winning all four major tournaments, he'll walk away from the game he loves. Against heavy odds Bobby wins the Grand Slam. He shares a hug with his father and grandfather, retires to be a full-time lawyer and family man, and designs the Augusta National Golf Club, the site of the esteemed annual tournament known as the Masters.

Before You Watch

Do you or your teen play golf? If so, schedule a round prior to your date night. Maybe you've never been on a course before. Why not give it a go and make a memory trying something new together? (Just be sure to take plenty of extra balls.) Alas, if you've been there, done that, and agree with Mark Twain that golf is "a good walk spoiled" you could always play a round of computer or miniature golf.

Bible Bookmarks

Prov. 3:5-6, 14:16-17, 16:32; Eph. 5:1-2; Phil. 2:3; Dan. 2:27-28; Isa. 42:16, 47:13-15

Talking Points

1. As a child Bobby is proficient at copying grownups, from golf swings to colorful language and club-throwing antics. It gets him into some bad habits. How can imitating people we respect do the same to us if we don't choose our role models carefully? Read Ephesians 5:1-2. Who are your role models? Why?

2.   Bobby's dad heaps pressure on him at an early age. Is that fair? Why or why not? How do you think Bobby felt? Have you ever felt that way? Can you relate to Bobby's confession to Mary that he felt "caged" by people's expectations of him? How so?

3.   Cite instances in which someone's faith in Bobby inspired him. Then ask your teen, "Is there an area of your life where you feel the need for more support than I've been giving you?" Talk about that. If possible, strive to be more encouraging in that area.

4.   Read Proverbs 14:16-17 and 16:32. Discuss Bobby's battle with anger and self-control. Do you know someone who loses his temper amid stress? How is that viewed by others? How would you describe your own temper?

5.   Read Philippians 2:3. What did Walter do or say that disrespected others? Compare that with how Bobby treated people. Talk about their different motivations, values, and priorities.

6.   Bobby quits during his first tournament at St. Andrews. Why is it nobler to lose than to quit? Have you ever experienced similar frustration? Did you press on or give up? Why? What did you learn from that?

7.   Talk about Bobby's decision to call a penalty on himself even though he could've gotten away with an imperceptible violation. Why did he do it? How did that make you feel toward him? What would you have done in that situation? In your own life, what things are "finer than winning championships"?

8.   How do you think Mary felt when put down by the snooty college girls? Have you ever felt inadequate in a group? Talk about that, as well as how Mary's sweet relationship with Bobby compares to dating relationships today.

9.   O. B. defends Bobby's amateur status, saying, "Money. It's gonna ruin sports." More than 75 years later, how have huge salaries, endorsement deals, and TV contracts impacted sports for good? For ill? Do you feel professional athletes are overpaid? Why or why not?

10. Early on, Bobby's mother refers to the Chinese zodiac. Later she says of her son, "His moon is in Sagittarius. He's in a very powerful cycle." What do Daniel 2:27-28 and Isaiah 47:13-15 say about putting stock in astrology?

11. O. B. quotes Will Rogers: "Good judgment comes from experience. And a lot of that comes from bad judgment." Bobby admits that he

28

never learned anything from winning a tournament. What have you learned from a mistake or defeat?

12. There's a fine line between pushing yourself to excel and applying so much pressure that you cease to enjoy what you're doing. Have you experienced this tug-of-war?

13. Walter says, "Three bad shots and one good one still make par. Golf is a game of recovery." How is life like that? Discuss how surrendering to Christ can be the one good shot that can turn things around (Isaiah 42:16, Proverbs 3:5-6). Name some people in the Bible who recovered well.

Follow-Up Activity

If you want to know more about the film and its subject, locate a copy of the book *Bobby Jones—Stroke of Genius: The Movie and the Man.*

The role of Stewart Maiden is played by respected pastor, author, and international evangelist Alistair Begg, heard on the radio program *Truth for Life.* If you've never heard him speak you can do so online by visiting truthforlife.org.

Just for Fun

Look closely at Mary's view from the trolley as Bobby tries to keep up with her on his bike. It's 1920, but reflections in the store windows behind him reveal a white minivan parked somewhere across the street. Oops!

—Bob Smithouser

29

The Day After Tomorrow

Rated: PG-13
Themes: Heroism, environmentalism, faith in God or man, teens boldly speaking truth, self-sacrifice, a father's love for his son
Running Time: 2 hours, 3 minutes
Starring: Dennis Quaid as Jack Hall; Jake Gyllenhaal as Sam Hall; Ian Holm as Dr. Rapson; Emmy Rossum as Laura; Sela Ward as Lucy Hall
Directed by: Roland Emmerich

Cautions

Two s-words are among the film's 20 profanities, with numerous exclamations of "oh god," "my god," etc. A man starts to unbutton his date's blouse. A shivering Sam (wearing only soaked boxers) huddles with Laura to avoid hypothermia. Intense situations of peril yield mass destruction and fatalities. While those deaths are handled discreetly, casualties and widespread devastation may upset younger viewers. Recommended for older teens and adults.

Story Summary

"Anything we can do to raise consciousness about the environment is a good thing. It's part of why we made this movie," said producer Mark Gordon.[1] Indeed, there's nothing subtle about *The Day After Tomorrow*'s if-we-don't-get-serious-about-global warming-we're-all-doomed political agenda. That's one reason we've included the film in this book; it offers mature viewers a way to explore Hollywood's knack for promoting a particular cause or worldview in the context of a high-octane popcorn flick. Another reason is its moral

31

characters and restraint, which are above average for a disaster movie.

We begin in Antarctica where renowned paleoclimatologist Jack Hall and his research team barely escape a huge ice quake. That close call heightens concerns that man's dependency on fossil fuels has accelerated global warming, melted polar ice caps, and desalinized the North Atlantic current. Jack warns world leaders (a callous American among them) that soon the phenomenon will wreak havoc on weather patterns, create catastrophic storms, and usher in a new ice age.

Just before nature unleashes its fury, Jack's estranged teenage son Sam flies to New York City for an academic competition accompanied by classmates, including his secret crush, Laura. Everything goes haywire. Tornadoes devastate Los Angeles. Large hail pounds Japan. A tidal wave engulfs Manhattan. Fortunately, Sam and others escape the marauding wall of water by holing up in the public library. A phone call to his parents arms Sam with the knowledge that the storm will worsen—and anyone caught outside will die. Jack insists that Sam stay put, promising to come for him.

The temperature drops dramatically, icing over New York's flooded streets. Most of the nation begins migrating south. So do many impatient people who sought refuge in the library along with Sam. Despite the teenager's pleas to wait it out, they brave the elements on foot and eventually perish. Those who stay behind forage for food and warm themselves by burning books. Laura takes ill, inspiring Sam and two friends to hunt for medicine aboard an abandoned Russian freighter that floated down Fifth Avenue before freezing in place. The boys must outrun the storm, as well as a pack of ravenous wolves.

In the meantime, Jack and two colleagues trek into the teeth of the storm in search of Sam, while Jack's physician wife chooses not to evacuate her post and remain alongside a sick child. Such selflessness is common, giving viewers plenty of people to root for on the way to a "happy" ending. For some unknown reason, the vicious superstorm stalls short of global annihilation. Meanwhile, father and son reunite, young love blossoms, and that grumpy vice president realizes the error of his ways.

NASA research oceanographer William Patzert said of *The Day After Tomorrow*, "The science is bad, but perhaps it's an opportunity to crank up the dialogue on our role in climate change."[2] Politicians including Al Gore hoped so. They timed speeches on global warming to coincide with the movie's release. One liberal advocacy group even recruited 8,000 volunteers to stand outside theaters and hand out brochures to moviegoers drawn in by the blockbuster's action, suspense, and eye-popping special effects.

Before You Watch

Arm yourselves with pads and pens. Then view the film with one eye focused on its environmental agenda. Note scenes and lines of dialogue that betray the filmmakers' attempt to portray global warming as a crisis demanding immediate attention, as well as their desire to vilify politicians who don't consider it a life-or-death priority.

Bible Bookmarks

1 Cor. 1:18-21; Jn. 15:13; Matt. 5:16, 25:31-40; Mk. 16:15-16; Col. 1:26; Lk. 19:10; Isa. 50:10-11; Gen. 1:28; Ps. 8

Talking Points

1. How does the story mix science fact and fiction to elicit a reaction about a real-life issue? Be specific. Refer to the notes you took during the movie. Help your teen realize that this motion picture wears its ambitions on its sleeve more than most, but that all films communicate the beliefs and values of the people behind them, sometimes in an attempt to affect our attitudes and behavior.

2. Read 1 Corinthians 1:18-21. In the library, Sam possesses lifesaving knowledge. When he shares it, some reject the truth and follow an authority figure to their doom. Others believe him and are saved. Draw as many parallels as you can to a Christian's need to share the gospel. What authority figures in our culture can lead people astray?

3. Ask, "Knowing only what the people in the library knew, what choice would you have made had you been there? Why?"

4. Catastrophe is a great equalizer. Discuss how wealth, gender, education, social status, etc. became less important amid tragedy. Then note how the homeless man, disrespected by society, made unique contributions to the group. Does your teen know someone being treated as a second-class citizen? Challenge him to identify that person's assets. Ask: "What can you do to make him/her feel more valuable?"

5. Talk about Lucy's decision to stay behind to comfort Peter, as well as Frank's self-sacrifice in order to spare his friends' lives, in light of John 15:13. What other acts of heroism impressed you?

6. Reflecting on her priorities and expectations for life, Laura sadly concludes, "Everything I've ever cared about, everything I've worked for has all been preparation for a future that no longer exists." Many people at the end of life have a similar epiphany. As Solomon reported in Ecclesiastes 1:14, most of what men pursue is "meaningless, a chasing after the wind." Help teens see the eternal significance in bringing God glory by saving and serving others (Matthew 5:16 and 25:31-40; Mark 16:15-16; Colossians 1:26).

7. What character in the film did you admire most? Why?

8. Jack embarks on a fantastic mission to save his child. No sacrifice is too great to restore their bond. Compare this to God's quest to redeem mankind (Luke 19:10). Note Sam's obedience to his father's words (taking a stand, not following the crowd) and his faith in his dad's ability to keep his promise ("He'll make it").

9. Sam fondly recalls a vacation gone bad because it gave him quality time with his dad. Has your family had a similar experience? If so, reminisce a little. If not, keep this in mind should it ever happen. Let it be a bonding experience rather than a source of frustration.

10. If you have the DVD, replay scene 24 ("The Age of Reason") and dissect the conversation about the Gutenberg Bible. What can we conclude about each person's faith? The humanistic Nietzsche fan reveres mankind's accumulated wisdom. Similarly, Jack later says, "Mankind survived the last Ice Age. We're certainly capable of surviving this one. It all depends on whether or not we're able to learn from our mistakes." What does Isaiah 50:10-11 say about people who misapply their trust this way?

Follow-Up Activity

The Bible calls us to be stewards of the earth and its resources (Genesis 1:28, Psalm 8). Plan another date with your teen that involves a simple journey into God's creation, be it a hike in the woods, a day on the lake, or a trek into the mountains. As you interact with nature, ponder a Christian's environmental duty. What does "subduing" the earth really mean? Might your family help out by planting trees, recycling, or taking part in a highway cleanup program? Also, consider how believers should respond to radical environmentalists, or pantheists who believe spirits indwell rocks, trees, and animals.

If you're curious about global warming, research the issue from different perspectives. Go online at epa.gov and click "global warming" for the stance of the U.S. Environmental Protection Agency. Some sites or blogs may express an alarmist view. Still others contend that it isn't nearly the crisis people make it out to be. One of those experts is climatologist Pat Michaels, who wrote the book *Meltdown: The Predictable Exaggeration of Global Warming by Scientists, Politicians and the Media.*

Just for Fun

Writer/director Roland Emmerich—a critic of George W. Bush's global warming policies—intentionally cast Kenneth Welsh as the stubborn V.P. because of the actor's resemblance to President Bush's second-in-command, Dick Cheney.

—Bob Smithouser

35

Down in the Delta

Rated: PG-13
Themes: Unconditional love, inner-city despair, substance abuse, the need for vision and hard work, tough love, preserving family legacy and unity, caring for a spouse with Alzheimer's
Running Time: 1 hour, 52 minutes
Starring: Alfre Woodard as Loretta Sinclaire; Mary Alice as Rosa Lynn; Wesley Snipes as Will; Al Freeman Jr. as Earl; Esther Rolle as Annie; Loretta Devine as Zenia
Directed by: Maya Angelou

Cautions

Precious few for a PG-13. There are a handful of profanities, including an s-word. A couple of Loretta's outfits reveal cleavage, and she frequently smokes cigarettes. The rating is for one scene in which Loretta and other addicts drink and do drugs in an abandoned apartment. Far from being offensive, this unglamorous depiction of a person ensnared in sin will send a powerful *anti*-drug message to young viewers.

Story Summary

As a matriarch, Rosa Lynn Sinclaire must feel like the captain of the *Titanic*. She cares for her autistic five-year-old granddaughter and battles to keep her preteen grandson, Thomas, away from Chicago's inner-city thugs while their apathetic single mom slides deeper into drugs and alcohol. Rosa Lynn's daughter, Loretta, is a tragic statistic waiting to happen. She gallivants all night and staggers in at

37

dawn. She ignores her little girl's basic needs and pawns family belongings to support her addictions. A failed job interview causes Loretta to hit rock bottom. A radical act of tough love may be the only lifeboat Rosa Lynn has left that can save her family.

Rosa Lynn phones her brother-in-law Earl, a hard-working Mississippi restaurant owner, and arranges for Loretta and the kids to spend the summer at the family's ancestral home down in the delta. Securing the bus fare requires a trip to a local pawn shop. With a steely glare and rock-solid resolve, Rosa Lynn pulls a sterling-silver candelabra named "Nathan" from a sack and starts haggling. Wide-eyed, Loretta can't believe her mother would sell this cherished family heirloom. It nets $375. Rosa Lynn hands the pawn ticket to Loretta and tells her she has until September 5 to earn enough money to buy Nathan back, placing a burden of responsibility on her that no one is sure she can handle.

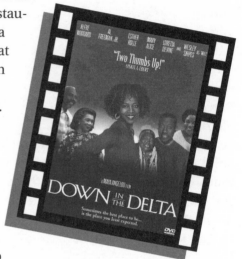

Upon arriving in rural Mississippi, Loretta has to adapt to a whole new way of life. Early mornings. Manual labor. Church on Sunday. She also must learn to accommodate her fading Aunt Annie, a victim of Alzheimer's lovingly cared for by Uncle Earl and their housekeeper, Zenia. "Maybe she should be in a home someplace," Loretta suggests. Earl patiently replies, "She *is* home." In the months that follow, Loretta witnesses his amazing tenderness and devotion toward his wife—a stark contrast to the selfish men in her world. Unfortunately, Annie's illness creates tension with Earl's son Will, a workaholic lawyer living in Atlanta who has trouble visiting a mother who doesn't recognize him.

Loretta's daily grind at Earl's restaurant involves stuffing sausages. She does it grudgingly at first. Then a visit to Zenia's modest home opens her eyes to new possibilities. Also a single mother of two, Zenia beams with pride at having a little place to call her own. Loretta sees hope. Meanwhile, Earl's unconditional love and faith in Loretta give her the incentive to change. Cracks form in her crusty exterior. With help from

38

her enterprising young son, Loretta learns enough math to become a waitress. More importantly, she realizes the value of having vision and taking personal responsibility for making good things happen in life.

Along the way, relationships deepen, including the one between Loretta and a certain candelabra. Earl tells stories of the Sinclaire family's roots that give her a more profound appreciation of her Civil War-era heritage. Thomas, too, is inspired by the discovery that he is part of a larger story. We eventually learn why the Sinclaires prize Nathan so. It seems Thomas's great, great, great grandfather Jesse was only six years old when he watched his master sell off a slave—Jesse's father, Nathan—in exchange for that candelabra. Jesse never saw his dad again. From one generation of Sinclaires to the next, Nathan served as a sterling-silver reminder to keep the family together at any cost. In the case of Rosa Lynn's desperate gamble, that totem of solidarity became a tool for making it possible.

Before You Watch

Start a casual family discussion about marriage vows. At the right moment, bring up the traditional phrases "in sickness and in health" and "till death do us part." Ask teens: "What do those lines mean to you? Is that realistic? Why or why not? What possible scenarios might you and your mate encounter? How do you think you'd respond if your spouse suffered a tragic illness or injury?" Remind them that God wants us to honor our vows, and is prepared to give us the strength and wisdom to do His will, no matter how difficult.

Bible Bookmarks

1 Pet. 5:8; Lk. 4:1-13, 8:12; 2 Cor. 11:14-15; Eph. 5:25, 6:11; Jas. 4:7; Col. 3:23-24

Talking Points

1. As Loretta finds out, sometimes a new routine and a change of scenery can help people break bad habits and develop healthier ones. Ask your teen if he or she wants to improve anything and what changes might help. (Example: A desire to eat smarter

39

might mean taking a route to and from school where there are no fast food restaurants.)

2.   One of Rosa Lynn's coworkers at the church notes, "The devil is strong, so strong." Turn to the Bible for a better understanding of Satan's power and his ploys (1 Peter 5:8, Luke 4:1-13 and 8:12, 2 Corinthians 11:14-15), and how Christians can protect themselves (Ephesians 6:11, James 4:7). Discuss how the devil uses people to corrupt other human beings.

3.   When Loretta refuses to leave the crack house, Rosa Lynn decides enough is enough. Have your teen put herself in the mother's place. Ask, "What other options did she have?" and "Can you think of places in the Bible where people's stubbornness forced God to get tough for their own good?"

4.   Talk about Earl's story of the rings on the tree trunk. How is the acknowledgment of our *spiritual* heritage similar to Thomas's revelation that he is part of a much bigger legacy? Why is that important?

5.   Referring to Annie's Alzheimer's, Zenia tells Loretta, "It's better to go with the madness than try to fight it." What does she mean? How can that philosophy improve our relationships? Are there ever times that we should fight the "madness"?

6.   How does Earl's selfless love for Annie fulfill Ephesians 5:25? Does your teen know someone with an incapacitating injury or disease that puts a heavy burden on his or her family members? Talk about that situation and compare it to the one in the film.

7.   Will was consumed with ambition, yet found it empty. Loretta's life was empty due to a *lack* of ambition. Clearly, neither extreme is healthy. What do you think is a good balance between the two? How does Colossians 3:23-24 apply?

8.   Loretta experiences a breakthrough when Earl says, "I guess you've seen and done some things that I never will understand. But you're a Sinclaire and that means something to us. I hope it means something to you." Earl acknowledges her sinful past, but instead of dwelling on it he emphasizes her *identity,* which is what connects them and makes her valuable. Explain how God's grace lets Him see us the same way.

 ## Follow-Up Activity

Zenia credits Habitat for Humanity with helping her to become a proud homeowner. Learn more about that fine organization by visiting habitat.org. Better yet, look for a building project in your area and volunteer. It would be a great chance to bond with your teen while helping a family in your community.

How much do you know about your ancestry? Encourage teens to interview their oldest living family member. Gather information for a family tree or a more exhaustive online search. You never know what will turn up. The main goal is to help adolescents realize that they are a chapter in a much larger story. As Christian recording artist Sara Groves states so eloquently in her song "Generations," it's easier for us to stand firm, morally, knowing we are the trusted link between our family's past and its future.

Just for Fun

Director Maya Angelou knows about stretching to fulfill one's potential against great odds. This best-selling author, poet, historian, playwright, actress, lecturer, and civil-rights activist was 70 when she directed *Down in the Delta,* her one and only feature film. This Renaissance woman told one interviewer she wanted to make a movie because, "Like all Americans, and probably all people by now, I've been formed and informed by film."

—Bob Smithouser

Eight Men Out

Rated: PG
Themes: Loyalty, honesty, temptation, rationalizing sin, peer pressure, integrity, compromise, gambling
Running Time: 2 hours
Starring: John Cusack as Buck; David Strathairn as Eddie; Charlie Sheen as Hap; D. B. Sweeney as Joe Jackson; John Mahoney as Kid Gleason
Directed by: John Sayles

Cautions

For a film with a PG rating, there's a lot of profanity. More than 30 instances include several s-words, a few misuses of the Lord's name and (inexplicably) an obscene gesture and one use of the term "f—up." Disappointing. Since this movie commonly airs on basic cable with much of this offensive content removed, we recommend recording and using the edited-for-TV version. Also expect some social drinking and tobacco use.

Story Summary

Why did the Chicago White Sox name their field Comiskey Park? It wasn't because of the former owner's generosity toward his players, that's for sure. In 1919 Charles Comiskey had the best team in baseball. A shoe-in to win the World Series. Yet while he treated the press to champagne and lavish post-game buffets, his players got table scraps. He even reneged on the bonus he'd promised them for winning the American League pennant. Resentment in the clubhouse set the stage for one of the most infamous scandals in the history of sports.

Gamblers knew the smart money would be on the Sox to dominate the Series, so they preyed on discontented players by bribing them to throw a few games. Once the athletes were in the gamblers' pockets, they had no recourse when told to take the ultimate dive.

According to the film, the first player to buy into the fix is Chick Gandil, a ham-fisted scoundrel with no allegiance to anyone but himself. Several others follow, including Chick's shady pal Swede. Still, the scam won't work without their pitching ace, Eddie Cicotte. Eddie turns Chick down cold just before meeting with Comiskey about a merit bonus that he clearly deserves, but is denied. Seeds of contempt sprout. What was unthinkable to Eddie a half-hour earlier is suddenly attractive. He's in. Hence, others sign on as well. But not Buck Weaver. The principled third baseman refuses to cheat.

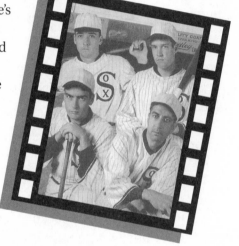

Throughout this process we see the plotting and conniving of the gamblers, a corrupt network of thugs, schemers, and kingpin financiers whose only love of the game is the payday it can yield. Scurrilous middle-men use money promised to the players to lay bets of their own. Chick and Swede add to their gamble by making the same dishonest deal with *two* sets of cons, hoping they won't find out about each other. Meanwhile, a few sports writers smell a rat.

Before long all of the compromised parties are losing sleep. The athletes are at each others' throats. Those on the take realize their poor play looks suspicious, but must insist they're doing their best. Two unexpected Sox victories cost the gamblers enough money that they can't pay the players what they need to keep them dishonest. With the team on the brink of elimination, a few ballplayers decide to start competing on the level, causing Arnold Rothstein's hoods to raise the stakes by threatening to kill Lefty's wife if he doesn't blow the final game.

What began as a quiet, vengeful jab at a stingy owner has snowballed. Everyone worries that they're in way over their heads. The Sox lose the series, but their troubles are just beginning. A journalist exposes

44

the dishonesty, leading to a grand jury investigation and a conspiracy trial. Although the defendants avoid jail time, each is banned from major league baseball by the newly appointed commissioner. That includes Buck Weaver and Shoeless Joe Jackson, two guys who played their hearts out yet pay the same heavy price.

As is so often the case, sin promises one thing and delivers another. After the trial is over and Chicago's heroes are proven to have feet of clay, Buck tells his young fans, "Don't be too down on the guys, fellas. When you grow up things get complicated." Must they? Temptations and mitigating circumstances may become more complex in adulthood, but basic ethics never change. In addition to being hailed as one of the best baseball movies ever, *Eight Men Out* illustrates how greed, resentment, and unfulfilled expectations can turn man's ear toward Satan's whispers.

 ## Before You Watch

In 2001, the gross revenues from legalized gambling were $68.7 billion. That's more money than Americans spent on music, movies, video games, theme parks, and sporting events combined. You could say it's our new national pastime. It's also a very different world for gamblers today than it was when wagering and corruption gave baseball a black eye in 1919. Invite your teen to talk about modern or high-tech gambling, their peers' attitudes toward it, and what they think of it, personally. For ideas about what to mention and how, explore helpful articles posted at family.org.

Bible Bookmarks

Rom. 12:17-21; Ps. 119:97-105; Lk. 4:1-13; Eph. 5:11, 6:10-18; Gal. 2:20; Heb. 9:22-28

Talking Points

1. How did bitterness toward Comiskey prime the players for what happened next? Consider specific ways resentment toward authority figures (teachers, bosses, politicians, etc.) can tempt people to cut corners. Read Romans 12:17-21 for a more appropriate response.

45

2. Chick and Swede possess fundamental character flaws. For Eddie, however, compromise emerges from a single weak emotional moment. Talk about his compromise, what led up to it, and what he might have done differently. Prepare for the moments of temptation we will all face by examining Christ's example (Luke 4:1-13) and our spiritual defenses (Psalm 119:97-105, Ephesians 6:10-18).

3. Lefty and Hap both rationalize their involvement because, since the outcome will be the same with or without them, why not cash in? Discuss why integrity isn't simply about affecting a result, but about *principle* regardless of the outcome.

4. Swede uses peer pressure to appeal to the uneducated Joe ("everyone's doing it"), then touches a nerve: "It would just be stupid not to do it. You don't want to be stupid, do you, Joe?" How can the enemy know and prey on our feelings of inadequacy? Point out that finding our identity in Christ—as in Galatians 2:20—can strengthen our resolve.

5. It's easy to view Buck as the noble one for not going along with the crowd, but how does his silence make him guilty? Was there ever a time when you didn't take part in something dishonest or inappropriate, yet failed to expose it? Apply Ephesians 5:11.

6. Put yourself in the shoes of White Sox manager Kid Gleason, the knickered young fans, or the players' wives. How might each feel a different sense of betrayal? Do you think the players' punishment fit the crime? Why or why not?

7. Buck's outburst in court finds him citing his performance, but he's destined to become a victim of the system since he lacks a special advocate. Share Hebrews 9:22-28. How is Buck like those who leave this world without the one, true Advocate, Jesus Christ?

8. If we equate the players to humans grappling with temptation, how can the network of gamblers symbolize the devil and his minions? Be as specific as possible. Consider Rothstein's wounded pride and how it led him to, as he told Abe, want to "own the game." What about the thugs and schemers who genuflect before him?

9. Early on Comiskey crows, "No room for prima donnas on this ball club. Every man for the good of the team." Is that the attitude in sports today? Why or why not? How does greed or selfishness continue to sabotage teams, companies, families, and ministries?

Follow-Up Activity

Take your teen to a baseball game. Buy some peanuts and Cracker Jacks. Root, root, root for the home team. Go with no agenda other than sharing a fun outing.

The timing of the Black Sox scandal could not have been worse for America, a nation trying to recover from WWI and headed into a depression. To learn more about the historical events depicted onscreen, visit chicagohs.org/history/blacksox.html together and see just how accurate the movie is. This site includes a detailed explanation of the scandal, photos of those involved, and explanations of what became of them later in life. Interested in complete statistics for the 1919 series? Go to blackbetsy.com/1919ws.htm.

Just for Fun

Joe Jackson got the nickname "Shoeless Joe" in 1908 while playing for a team in Greenville, South Carolina. A new pair of spikes had worn painful blisters on his feet. Although he had hoped to sit out the next road game, his team was shorthanded. It was either hurt in the new cleats or play in stocking feet. After Joe hit a triple a fan drew attention to his lack of footwear and the name stuck.

—Bob Smithouser

Emma

Rated: PG
Themes: Finding a soul mate, meddling in romance, propriety, honesty in friendship, charity, humility, honoring social conventions, taming the tongue, forgiveness
Running Time: 2 hours, 1 minute
Starring: Gwyneth Paltrow as Emma Woodhouse; Toni Collette as Harriet Smith; Jeremy Northam as John Knightley; Alan Cumming as Mr. Elton; Greta Scacchi as Mrs. Weston
Directed by: Douglas McGrath

Cautions

Incidental social drinking and two exclamations of "good god."

Story Summary

This romantic comedy about a misguided young match-maker is based on Jane Austen's 1816 novel of the same name. The author's calculating cupid is Emma Woodhouse, a socially privileged 21-year-old woman who proclaims, "The most beautiful thing in the world is a match well made." Emma feels it's her job to pair up acquaintances, convinced she understands their hearts better than they do. It's her calling. Her duty. Truth be known, it's more of an obsessive hobby and she's not very good at it. Emma is clueless about what constitutes true love and ends up reducing romance to a caste-driven formula aided by a heavy dose of her own vain intuition.

Emma takes place in Highbury, England, over a year's time. The story line is essentially a tangled web of gentle manipulation, misread signals, petty jealousies, and awkward interactions that conclude with the title character experiencing life-changing revelations about matters of the heart. Rather than breaking down those complex relationships chronologically, let's take a look at key characters and their impact on Emma's world:

Mrs. Weston—Formerly Miss Taylor, this newlywed was Emma's governess and respected friend. After 16 years of motherly devotion to Emma, she recently left the Woodhouse estate to marry a widower and start a family of her own (a match for which Emma takes credit). More a peer than a guardian, her departure still saddens Emma, though Mrs. Weston remains a dear confidante.

Mr. Knightley—The big brother Emma never had, he has been her most caring and forthright male friend for years. He's a true gentleman, both sensible and chivalrous, and would be a good match for Emma if her respect for him were less platonic. Knightley's brother John is married to Emma's sister Isabelle.

Mr. Elton—The local vicar is Emma's latest "project." But she is unaware that this self-impressed bachelor's deep longings are for *her*, not for Harriet, the young woman she has been dangling in front of him. Upon learning that Emma doesn't return his affection, Mr. Elton shocks everyone by marrying a domineering snob prone to self-flattery.

Harriet Smith—A sweet, rather simple newcomer to Highbury, she's forced to take the long road to love because of Emma's well-intentioned meddling. Emma sabotages the shy girl's attraction to a noble farmer in order to match her with Mr. Elton. After that attempt goes bust, Harriet endures another romantic disappointment before ending up back in the farmer's arms.

Miss Bates—This guileless spinster cares for her aging mother, never missing a chance to chatter away about nothing in particular. Her nervous streams of consciousness grate on Emma, though Mr. Knightly shows Miss Bates uncommon patience and compassion.

Frank Churchill—Frank is Mr. Weston's son, raised from infancy by an aunt and uncle in London. The impishly cavalier young man's first trip to Highbury involves great fanfare and mild flirtations with Emma—even though he is secretly engaged.

Jane Fairfax—She is Miss Bates's lovely niece, an enigmatic woman of few words who pays her aunt a much-anticipated visit midway through the film. Emma doesn't think much of Jane, treating her with suspicion and viewing her as a potential rival.

Once again, Jane Austen *(Sense and Sensibility, Pride and Prejudice)* shows how human emotions, class expectations, and social norms made life in early nineteenth-century England complicated and unpredictable. Not that things are so different for young people today. In fact, the 1995 movie *Clueless* borrows heavily from *Emma* and repopulates Austen's story with Southern California teens in modern (often inappropriate) situations. In both cases the heroine learns that true love must take its own course . . . in its own time. And the best matches rarely conform to a romantic ideal.

Before You Watch

Does your teen discuss finding a soul mate? Although most adolescents aren't in any hurry to marry, they've probably developed some romantic ideals. Without being critical of those notions, initiate a conversation about the kind of person they hope to marry. Focus on character traits and why they seem important. What attributes would your teen rather *avoid?* After watching the film, see if any of the characters model your teen's priorities.

Bible Bookmarks

Prov. 4:23, 16:2, 21:23, 27:2 and 27:6; 1 Cor. 13:7; Eph. 4:15; Jas. 3:3-12; 1 Pet. 5:5-6

Talking Points

1. While preparing to write *Emma*, Jane Austen noted that she was going to create "a heroine whom no one but myself will much like."[3] How do you feel about Emma? Did specific scenes alter your opinion of her along the way?

2. Read Proverbs 16:2. Although Emma doesn't think of her scheming as cruel, how is her behavior similar to "mean girl" manipulation in high schools today? What was it about the women's personalities and social stations that made it possible for Emma to influence Harriet as she did?

3. The thrill of the challenge distracted Emma from focusing on the individual needs of the people she was "helping." As Christians, if we're not careful, how can we do the same to those we minister to? (Example: "winning" converts vs. investing in lives)

4. Harriet was perfectly happy with Robert Martin until Emma planted doubts in her mind and made her think the grass was greener somewhere else. What voices disrupt our contentment that way? Apply Proverbs 4:23 and discuss practical ways to "guard your heart."

5. What about Mr. Knightley made him a good catch? Is it realistic to hold out for mates with those character traits today? Why or why not? Also, why is a friendship tested by time a good foundation for marriage?

6. The Eltons are quite a pair. Describe your opinion of Mr. Elton based on things he said and did. Mrs. Elton pretends to be modest about her talents but never fails to praise herself via her "friends." Why do you think she does that? Read Proverbs 27:2 and 1 Peter 5:5-6. What is real humility?

7. At the picnic, Emma makes a cruel joke at Miss Bates's expense. Who ends up looking worse? Why? How does Emma's faux pas illustrate Proverbs 21:23 and James 3:3-12? Do you know someone who would rather get a laugh with a put-down than offer a kind word? Retracting careless comments can be like trying to refill a toothpaste tube. Have you ever said something you wished you could take back?

8. Discuss the difference between "charity" and "kindness." What does Mr. Knightley mean when he assures an ashamed Emma, "The truest friend does not doubt, but hope" (a reflection of 1 Corinthians 13:7)?

9. Apply Proverbs 27:6 and Ephesians 4:15 to Mr. Knightley's rebukes of Emma. In your own words, what does it mean to "speak truth in love"? Whose opinion of you matters enough that you would take his or her criticism to heart? Why is that relationship so valuable?

10. One reason Mr. Knightley scolds Emma is because she made the remark in front of "people who would be guided by" her treatment of Miss Bates. Do respected role models have a greater responsibility to

watch what they say and do? Why or why not? How does this apply to athletes, entertainers, or other celebrities today?

11. Churchill and Knightley both come to the rescue of ladies in need. Talk about how their acts of chivalry differ. Which of the men made the greater sacrifice?

12. Analyzing her feelings for Frank, Emma muses, "I felt listless after he left, and had some sort of headache, so I must be in love as well. I must confess, I expected love to feel somewhat different than this." Describe romantic feelings you've experienced. Were they what you expected? What leads us to form those expectations?

Follow-Up Activity

To people in Emma's culture, receiving a letter was a big deal. They couldn't wait to share news of loved ones with family and friends. In our age of e-mails and text messaging, letter-writing has become a lost art. But for some people today (missionaries, prisoners, nursing home residents, homesick college students) getting a letter would still be a special event. Set aside an evening with your teen and each of you hand-write a letter to someone God puts on your heart.

Just for Fun

Since portraying Frank Churchill in *Emma,* Ewan McGregor has become known for wielding a lightsaber as young Obi Wan Kenobi in *Star Wars: Episodes I, II,* and *III.* But did you know that McGregor first caught the acting bug from his uncle, Dennis Lawson, who played Luke Skywalker's pilot pal Wedge Antilles in the original *Star Wars* trilogy?

—Bob Smithouser

Father of the Bride

Rated: PG
Themes: Releasing a grown child, adjusting to life changes, expanding a family and embracing in-laws, unconditional love and acceptance, wedding chaos, family memories, parental sacrifice
Running Time: 1 hour, 45 minutes
Starring: Steve Martin as George Banks; Diane Keaton as Nina Banks; Kimberly Williams as Annie; Martin Short as Franck; George Newbern as Bryan MacKenzie
Directed by: Charles Shyer

Cautions

There's some alcohol use (beer, wine, champagne) and several exclamations of "oh my god." At one point, George and Nina seem resigned to the fact that unmarried couples have sex. George nervously tells Annie and Bryan as they head out for a drive, "Don't forget to fasten your condom—*seat belt*." Later, Nina reminds her husband that they'd been intimate numerous times in her parents' house.

Story Summary

George Banks considers love and matrimony wonderful things . . . until they happen to his only daughter, 22-year-old Annie. He looks forward to her return from Rome where she has spent four months studying architecture. Although George is a successful businessman, his first love is his family and the Southern California home where they've created precious memories together. Playing basketball in the driveway. Teaching his children to ride bikes. Pitching tents in the backyard. Seeing young Annie slide down the banister. George is a contented man about to get a life-changing surprise.

Annie has returned from Rome looking more grown up. During dinner, she drops the bombshell that she's engaged to Bryan, a young computer genius she met abroad. Her mom, Nina, listens excitedly to her news, but George is shocked and suspicious of this young stranger poised to take his place as Annie's hero. Instead of seeing the woman his daughter has become, he still imagines a seven-year-old with pigtails. George realizes he has reached that fearful place "when you quit worrying about her meeting the wrong guy and you worry about her meeting the *right* guy . . . because that's when you lose her."

George's vocal lack of support drives Annie from the dinner table. Nina chides him to go after her and apologize, which he does. He sets aside pessimism and sarcasm long enough to play a spirited game of one-on-one with his little girl and brace for meeting her fiancé. The young man turns out to be charming, though it's clear that, in George's mind, no one would be good enough for Annie. His negativity extends beyond Bryan to everything related to the engagement. Bryan's wealthy parents. The length of the guest list. Nina putting the kibosh on his idea of holding the wedding at the Steak Pit. The truth is, it's tough for this aging dad to release his daughter into adulthood. His role has always been to protect her, advise her, worry about her, and care for her needs. Now another man is stepping in.

When George finally accepts the inevitable, this crazy ride picks up speed. With the help of a flamboyant, nearly unintelligible wedding coordinator named Franck, the blessed event threatens to turn his emotions and pockets inside out. George struggles to keep his cool amid complications and ballooning costs. Just when he makes peace with the whole thing, a lover's quarrel between Annie and Bryan threatens to end the engagement. It seems Bryan's gift of a blender is an affront to Annie's feminist ideals, and it's up to Dad to smooth over the rough spots. Soon the wedding is back on.

The night before the ceremony, Annie and her father chat about her own odd feelings. She's excited about marriage, but the transition is bittersweet. Home won't be home anymore. (While most of the story is told from George's perspective in a way that allows young viewers to appreciate what a parent goes through, this moment helps adults understand adolescent anxiety.) As unexpected snowflakes begin to fall, Annie also fears that inclement weather will cost her father even more money. But George has surrendered everything to forces beyond his control. Now he's focusing on what's truly important. He tells Annie, "I know I'll remember this moment for the rest of my life." Despite some challenges, the wedding is a success and George discovers that the special love between a father and daughter can never be replaced.

Before You Watch

If you have a teenage daughter, buy a few bridal magazines and flip through them together. Find out what styles she finds appealing, and by extension some of her dreams for that special day. Cut out favorite photos and paste them in a notebook, or make a collage that you can reflect upon when she actually gets engaged. By looking at those magazines, gather a sense of what the editors consider important about weddings. Do you agree? Also, talk about why brides wear white, and relate that to previous discussions of sexual purity (1 Corinthians 6:18-20).

Bible Bookmarks

Eph. 5:21-33; Phil. 4:6-7; Jer. 29:11; Mk. 10:7-9; Prov. 22:6; Isa. 26:3, 43:2; 1 Cor. 13 and 6:18-20

Talking Points

1. George talks about life's surprises and how they can sneak up and grab hold of us. Have you encountered any surprises lately? Have circumstances challenged your expectations? Take comfort in scriptures such as Philippians 4:6-7, Jeremiah 29:11,

Isaiah 26:3 and 43:2, which can keep us from overreacting as George did.

2. George admits that he's "not a guy who's big on change." How does his refusal to go with the flow compound his problems? Can you relate? What eventually changes his attitude?

3. Playing basketball is a bonding activity for the Banks family. What's yours? Do you have favorite memories of things your family has done together? How has your home played a role in those memories?

4. Read 1 Corinthians 13. In describing their affection for one another, what did Bryan and Annie say that proved that their love was unselfish? Invite your teen to describe the qualities they plan to hold out for in a mate. Ask, "How much input should a parent have in who their child marries?"

5. Annie says that, until she met Bryan, she "didn't believe in marriage," fearing it would cost her her identity and play into pre-feminist social politics. How has our culture changed its attitude toward marriage—for better or worse—since the 1950s? Read Ephesians 5:21-33 for a biblical view of love and submission intended by God to strengthen marriages.

6. Bryan's dad says, "Sooner or later you just have to let your kids go and hope you brought 'em up right." Proverbs 22:6 seems to agree. Ask your teen, "What things have I done *well* to prepare you for life on your own? Is there anything I could do better?"

7. Annie describes the weird feeling of spending her last night in the house where she grew up ("Kinda like my last night as a kid. . . . It was so strange packing up my room"). Yet "leaving and cleaving" is part of marriage (Mark 10:7-9). Ask, "What frightens you about the thought of leaving home someday? What about it appeals to you?" Talk about your own transition into independence and share significant lessons you learned.

8. Sensitive to the fact that his preoccupation with the wedding has interfered with Matty's father-son time, George wants to make it up to him. Are you so focused on something that you've let relationships slide? What can you do to remind those people how valuable they are?

9. Separately, come up with five adjectives to describe Annie's and George's father-daughter bond, then compare your lists. What aspects of their relationship do you admire? Do parents and children always have to agree in order to have a good relationship? Why or why not?

10. In jail, George promises Nina, "I will try to remember my daughter's feelings, and how with every roll of my eyes I am taking away a piece of her happiness." We can disrespect each other with nonverbal expressions even when we'd never use hurtful words. Do you ever do that? Discuss those habits and how you might communicate more respectfully to each other.

Follow-Up Activity

Pull out photo albums and talk about your own courtship, engagement, and wedding day. Special memories. Pleasant surprises. Humorous things that went wrong. What did the process of planning that important day teach you about your spouse and members of your extended family? Help your teen understand that an elaborate, romantic ceremony and reception shouldn't be the ultimate goal, but rather a spiritually grounded beginning for a lifelong journey.

Just for Fun

Annie and Bryan get an early wedding gift of a Venus de Milo statue with a clock in its stomach. It's a subtle homage to the original *Father of the Bride* (1950), starring Spencer Tracy and Elizabeth Taylor, which featured the same tacky present. Also, keep an eye on George's socks, which are white in the supermarket but black in jail. Oops!

—Lissa Halls Johnson

Finding Neverland

Rated: PG
Themes: Growing up yet staying young at heart, the power of imagination, faith in others, friendship, hope, propriety vs. playfulness, healthy hedges in marriage, coping with loss
Running Time: 1 hour, 41 minutes
Starring: Johnny Depp as J. M. Barrie; Kate Winslet as Sylvia Llewelyn Davies; Julie Christie as Mrs. Emma du Maurier; Radha Mitchell as Mary Ansell Barrie; Dustin Hoffman as Charles Frohman; Freddie Highmore as Peter
Directed by: Marc Forster

Cautions
A few crass British phrases are used.

Story Summary
It's opening night. A restless gathering of buttoned-down British socialites waits for the curtain to rise on playwright J. M. Barrie's latest work. High expectations have the author pacing in the wings. Then, as the actors strut and fret in their hour upon the stage, Barrie realizes it's a flop. He graciously greets an unimpressed public and gathers encouragement from his loyal producer, who is confident he'll bounce back.

That rebound begins in the summer of 1903 when Barrie's aristocratic wife, Mary, declines an invitation to join him for his daily stroll in the park. She knows his mind will be on work. It seems Mary wed an eccentric artist and, now aware of the downside, is frustrated. He is

61

equally alienated by the aloof propriety that keeps her from joining him in his whimsical world. That divergence is accelerated when, during his visit to the park, Barrie stumbles upon young brothers playing make believe. He joins them and meets their recently widowed mother, Sylvia Llewelyn Davies. Daily encounters lead to a sweet, platonic friendship.

Barrie's kind heart and gamesmanship stimulate the four siblings' already vivid imaginations.

The playwright becomes a puckish father figure to the boys who, in turn, serve as his muse. Young Peter is especially intriguing. He lacks the fun-loving abandon of his brothers, seeing things through more literal, jaded eyes. In short, he's growing up too fast. That troubles Barrie. It also inspires him to craft a new, wildly unortho-dox play about a lad who *refuses* to grow up. Wild Indians. Fairies. Mermaids. A ticking crocodile. They, along with bloodthirsty pirates, inhabit a magi-cal place called Neverland. At the center of his surreal fable is a scalawag named Peter Pan.

As preproduction on this risky theatrical venture commences, Sylvia stubbornly refuses treat-ment for an undiagnosed illness. She suspects it's serious yet doesn't want to waste away in a hospital bed like her husband did. The more her health deteriorates, the more time Barrie spends with the Llewelyn Davies clan and away from his wife, who resents his priorities. Sylvia's strict, patrician mother also opposes Barrie's investment in her family. The proud matriarch obsesses that Barrie's presence is providing grist for the local rumor mill, which it is.

Soon *Peter Pan* opens to rave reviews, thanks in part to a gaggle of orphans planted in the crowd to loosen up the stuffy elite. But the play's success is bittersweet. Barrie's wife leaves him for another man. And Sylvia's time is short. In a grand gesture of compassion, Barrie and his cast take the play to his housebound friend, giving her and the boys a taste of Neverland and a glittery sliver of hope. "You taught us we could change things by believing them to be different," Sylvia tells him. Sadly, positive thinking isn't always enough. Sylvia dies, and Barrie agrees to help raise the boys.

"The screenplay I wrote is not a factual retelling of what happened to James Barrie when he wrote *Peter Pan*," says screenwriter David Magee. "I wanted to tell a story about what it means to grow up and become responsible for those around you. I hope people see the film as a respectful tribute to Barrie's creative genius and come away with a feeling that as human beings, we can grow up without losing all aspects of childhood innocence and wonder."

Finding Neverland accomplishes that goal beautifully, though parents and teens can go further. In the film, innocence and wonder become a feel-good balm for dealing with heavy issues. Life. Death. Youth. Belief. Priorities. Eternity. Fortunately, Christians can reach beyond the humanistic substitute of mere imagination and find true hope in the character of God and the assurance of heaven.

Before You Watch

If your teen has never seen *Peter Pan*, or if all they know is Disney's animated musical, find a live-action version and watch it together. The 2003 film starring Jeremy Sumpter and Jason Isaacs is a pretty good one (clearly aimed at a preteen audience, so prepare teenagers that it may seem a bit beneath them). Or you could read the play exactly as Barrie wrote it. Either way, a familiarity with the story will make *Finding Neverland* much more meaningful.

Bible Bookmarks

Lk. 14:12-14; Acts 4:36; Matt. 5:31-32, 23:11-12; Mk. 10:35-45; Jas. 1:27, 4:13-17; Eph. 5:15-17, 5:25; Ps. 89:47-48; Jn. 10:10, 14:1-4; Rev. 21-22

Talking Points

1. Discuss Barrie's disdain for the word "just" as a weapon used to keep someone or something from fulfilling its creative potential (e.g., "It's just a dog" rather than a dancing bear). What does he

63

mean? Do you agree? Ask, "What did Barrie need to ignite his creativity? What do *you* need to express yours?" Offer to help make that happen.

2. Apply Luke 14:12-14 to the Barries' different motives for inviting Sylvia's family to dinner. How can this lesson relate to your own lives?

3. When Michael struggles to get the kite in the air, Barrie yells, "It's not going to work if no one believes in him!" How is that true elsewhere in life? Do you know someone facing a daunting task who needs encouragement? How can you be a modern-day Barnabas to that person (Acts 4:36)?

4. Barrie's cricket mate states, "Once you get a bit of notoriety, James, people watch you, and they will look for ways to drag you down." How is that true of celebrities today? (Share specific examples: supermarket tabloids, malicious paparazzi, hateful Web sites, etc.) Why do you think this happens?

5. Sylvia's mother and Mary are both obsessed with propriety and social status. How does that rob them of joy and peace? Do you know anyone so busy trying to impress others or maintain an image that they miss out on life's simple pleasures? What advice would you offer them? How is this relevant to Jesus' teaching in Matthew 23:11-12 and Mark 10:35-45?

6. How were the Barries' goals and personalities mismatched? Our culture might consider that sufficient grounds for divorce. Why isn't it according to Matthew 5:31-32? What could each spouse have done differently to help improve the marriage?

7. Was J. M. Barrie right to spend so much time with the Llewelyn Davies family? Why or why not? How might he have helped that family *and* respected healthy boundaries at home? Explore how he mismanaged the noble deeds described in Ephesians 5:25 and James 1:27, erring toward the latter which happened to be more personally rewarding. How can devotion to a "good" thing keep us from making the "best" choice?

8. The elderly woman at the play remarks, "It's all the work of the ticking crocodile, isn't it? Time is chasing after all of us." Ponder the brevity of life and how we should redeem each day (James 4:13-17, Ephesians 5:15-17, Psalm 89:47-48).

9. Consider Peter's tirade about wanting to deal honestly with life's trials. Is that necessarily a bad thing? Discuss the tension between preserving youthful innocence and imagination, and the need to (as George did) confront adult matters maturely. At what point does retreating into make-believe become counterproductive? (Example: Neverland is a

substitute for heaven for those unaware of, or disinclined to rely on God's promises. Explain that God has hardwired us to yearn for the sweet hereafter described in John 14:1-4 and Revelation 21-22, and that the world has many counterfeits that lull people into a false, Christ-less sense of security.)

10. Why did Sylvia refuse treatment for her sickness? Do you agree with her decision?

11. Stodgy adults find the joy in *Peter Pan* only after viewing it through the orphans' eyes and sharing their delight. Likewise, the abundant joy Jesus promises in John 10:10 can be experienced only when we see the world and others through God's eyes. Name some practical ways you can do that.

Follow-Up Activity

This delicate biopic takes significant liberties with Barrie's story for feel-good effect. To learn more about the details behind *Peter Pan,* pick up Andrew Birkin's book *J. M. Barrie and the Lost Boys.*

Just for Fun

To loosen up the boys during the scene at the dinner table, Johnny Depp planted a flatulence machine under Julie Christie's chair and kept setting it off by remote control. The spoon trick isn't bad, but now you know what the kids were *really* laughing at.

—*Bob Smithouser*

Fly Away Home

Rated: PG
Themes: Father-daughter bonding, teamwork, adopting a noble cause, losing parents to divorce or death, duty to wildlife, healing, humility
Running Time: 1 hour, 47 minutes
Starring: Jeff Daniels as Tom Alden; Anna Paquin as Amy Alden; Dana Delany as Susan Barnes; Terry Kinney as Uncle Dave
Directed by: Carroll Ballard

Cautions

Though bloodless and silent, the opening scene features a roll-over accident that takes the driver's life. Expect a few mild profanities and exclamatory uses of "my god." There's one s-word late in the film (hit mute just as Amy's aircraft buzzes the hunters). Tom bolts out of the house wearing only bikini briefs. A showering girl is seen, obscured, through clouded glass.

Story Summary

As we hear the haunting strains of Mary Chapin Carpenter's song "10,000 Miles," a mother and daughter get forced off the road somewhere in New Zealand. Only the 13-year-old girl survives the crash, and awakens in a hospital bed with her estranged father by her side. Amy hasn't seen him since her parents' divorce nine years earlier. Now he's her guardian.

Tom Alden takes his daughter back to rural Ontario and the home they once shared. The scruffy inventor/artist clearly loves Amy and wants to ease her grief. Still, he's an eccentric up to his ears in work.

67

When he's not welding scales onto an iron dragon, he's strapping on a homemade glider and taking to the skies. Amy thinks he's nuts. Actually, he's nuts about *her* and eager to reconnect. But she doesn't make it easy. Sarcastic remarks toward Tom and his girlfriend, Susan, create distance.

One day the tranquility of dawn is rudely interrupted by the belching and grinding of a bulldozer clearing marsh land in the name of progress. The intrusion displaces a flock of geese, leaving a nest full of eggs in need of care. Amy secretly gathers them up, builds a makeshift incubator, and waits for them to hatch. Once they do, they imprint with her as they would their mother. The fuzzy little goslings follow her everywhere. But what will happen when they need to migrate? Geese survive by mimicking their own kind. A well-intentioned wildlife officer makes the mistake of trying to enforce an ordinance by clipping their wings. Amy and Tom rise to the birds' defense and drive him off.

Father and daughter become united by a cause. Tom promises he won't let anyone hurt the geese. So does Susan, who tells Amy, "I can never replace your mother. . . . But if you let me, I can be your friend." Amy opens up. She also warms to her goofy Uncle Dave, Tom's visiting brother. However, the biggest breakthrough is with Dad. By making what's important to his daughter important to him, Tom demonstrates how much he cares. He hatches a plan to use his ultralight plane to guide Amy's birds on a migratory path south.

Aided by visual cues and engine sounds, the birds get comfortable enough to trail a one-man aircraft. But only if Amy is at the controls. So Tom sells his prized possession to buy the safest, easiest-to-fly model available. He trains Amy to fly behind him and lead the geese. Before long they have a flight plan and a deadline. If they can make it to a wetlands region of North Carolina by November 1, not only will Amy's geese have a safe winter home, but they'll be rescuing what's left of a sanctuary about to be bulldozed by developers. The honorable journey turns Amy into a media darling. More importantly, it's a rite of passage that bonds father and daughter.

Film critic Roger Ebert writes, "All of this sounds, I suppose, like a daffy retread of *Free Willy* or one of those other movies in which small children befriend noble animals. But *Fly Away Home* is not quite that simple. . . . The film [is] visually uplifting, and the story is quirky enough and the dialogue so fresh and well-acted that this film rises above its genre."[4] Indeed, gorgeous cinematography and Ballard's smart approach to the material make this a nuanced, inspirational family film. Anna Paquin (between winning an Oscar and playing Rogue in the *X-Men* movies) is likable and authentic here as the aimless, hurting girl who finds her way, not by brooding, but by looking beyond herself and serving others.

Before You Watch

Track down a copy of the Christian book *Why Geese Fly Farther Than Eagles* by Bob Stromberg. Turn to the poem on pages 13-18 for a great lesson about teamwork that will also deepen your family's appreciation of how God designed geese for migration.

Bible Bookmarks

Phil. 2:4-8; Prov. 3:5-6, 12:26; Josh. 1:8; 2 Tim. 3:16-17; Lk. 22:27; Jn. 13:14; 1 Cor. 10:24; Rom. 13:1; Ps. 119:9-11, 119:105

Talking Points

1. What did you think when you saw Amy flying? Were you more nervous for her safety or envious of her opportunity? Was it responsible of Tom to put his daughter in a plane like that? Why or why not?

2. How was Amy, like the geese, in need of someone to show her the way in life? Why is it important to be careful whom we follow? Read Proverbs 12:26, then discuss the need to use God's Word as our primary guide (Joshua 1:8, Proverbs 3:5-6, 2 Timothy 3:16-17, Psalm 119:9-11, 119:105).

3. What impressed you most about how everyone banded together

to save the geese? Have you ever found yourself caring for a homeless or injured animal? What happened, and how did it make you feel?

4. Amy is visibly displeased that Susan sometimes lives with her father. Talk about the moral issue of cohabitating outside of marriage, and why God disapproves of it. For a practical, biblical view of the issue, scan the articles at troubledwith.com (search "cohabitation").

5. Building the scale model of the Lunar Lander had been the final straw that sent Tom's family packing. Selling it became a catalyst for restoration with Amy. Why? What did that creation symbolize, and why was his decision to part with it so significant?

6. The ranger comes across as the bad guy, but isn't a typical screen villain. How is he different? Put yourself in his place. Did he have other options? Do you think the Aldens overreacted? Apply Romans 13:1.

7. What do the filmmakers think of nature? Of land developers? Explain whether you feel it was fair to portray developers so negatively. Can you think of a reasonable compromise between *using* the land and *preserving* it?

8. Late in the film Amy gets a nose ring, which doesn't seem to bother her dad. How does your family feel about body piercing? What's acceptable? How much is too much?

9. Amy expresses her mother's opinion that artists can be selfish, which apparently hurt the marriage between her (a singer) and Tom (an inventor/sculptor). Why might creative people have a harder time with selfishness? Have you struggled with it? How?

10. Read Luke 22:27, John 13:14, and 1 Corinthians 10:24. How did father and daughter each find healing by turning their attention to the needs of others? Are you struggling with personal pain? Maybe relief is as close as your decision to focus less on that issue and more on what you can do for others. Consider ways you might do that.

11. Whether or not you agree with the filmmakers' bias, there's no denying that they use images and characterizations to guide the audience's rooting interest. (Example: creating warmth and sympathy for a struggling family while portraying the developers as an ominous, generally faceless "force.") They pit cold, marauding construction equipment against a cute, motherless girl and orphaned birds. Not hard to pick sides, right? Role-play for a moment. Hollywood is offering you millions for a script that makes prospective homeowners/developers sympathetic

and vilifies stubborn environmentalists. Together, brainstorm ideas that would tell *that* story.

Follow-Up Activity

Most parents can identify with Tom's exasperation in attempting to reach Amy ("I've tried everything. I've been nice to her. I've been tough on her. Nothing's worked."). Success came when he set aside his own pursuits long enough to make her priorities his own. What's important to your teen? Look for ways to get out of your comfort zone and connect at a level that will be meaningful to him or her. It's humbling, effective, and Christlike (Philippians 2:4-8).

If you're intrigued by the "imprinting" process, rent the beautiful wildlife feature *Winged Migration*—and don't miss the "making of" bonus material. Fascinating!

Just for Fun

From 1989-92, Dana Delany earned four Best Actress Emmy nominations for her role as Army nurse Colleen McMurphy on the ABC drama *China Beach* (she won twice). Not too shabby. But it was her grandfather, John, who *really* changed the world by inventing the Delany Valve, a flushing mechanism still used in modern toilets (see it at coynedelany.com/features.htm). Coincidentally, Dana's character in *Fly Away Home* is dating an inventor.

—*Bob Smithouser*

71

The Incredibles

Rated: PG
Themes: Family unity, teamwork, embracing one's true identity, striving for excellence vs. accepting mediocrity, midlife crisis, marital trust and fidelity, revenge, redemption, teen angst, common heroism
Running Time: 1 hour, 55 minutes
Starring: The voices of Craig T. Nelson as Mr. Incredible; Holly Hunter as Elastigirl; Jason Lee as Syndrome; Samuel L. Jackson as Frozone; Brad Bird as Edna Mode
Directed by: Brad Bird

Cautions

For teens they're minor. Mainly action violence, scenes of children in peril, two exclamations of "my god," and a reference to a drinking game.

Story Summary

Mr. Incredible is at the top of his game. Uniquely gifted. Publicly adored. Professionally fulfilled. The spandex-clad superhero prides himself on being a lone-ranger defender of justice (much to the chagrin of Buddy, an obsessed young fan eager to become his sidekick). Everything's super. Then the unthinkable happens. Just as Mr. Incredible is tying the knot with his rubber-limbed love Elastigirl, we learn that noble mishaps have led to so many lawsuits against the city that Metroville's superheroes are being forced into early retirement. A government relocation program will set them up with normal jobs and normal lives under the condition that they stop being super.

73

We next encounter Bob and Helen Parr 15 years later in suburban midlife, suppressing their powers and trying to remain as average and ordinary as their new name implies. Helen is stretched to the limit raising three children, including a lightning-fast little boy (Dash), a brooding teenage daughter prone to invisibility and erecting force fields (Violet), and a new baby capable of who knows what. Meanwhile, Bob rescues old ladies from the bureaucratic red tape of his employer, a chintzy insurance company. Instead of saving the world with his ultra strength, he now hears his wife say, "Go save the world one policy at a time, honey!" These days Mr. Incredible's greatest nemeses are a receding hairline, bulging gut, and intense boredom. On the sly, he and his pal Lucius (formerly the icy hero Frozone) listen to a police scanner while reliving their glory days. But things are about to change.

A loss of self-control costs Bob his job. Then a holographic message from a mysterious woman invites him to don his old super suit to corral a renegade robot on a remote island. Bob secretly accepts the mission and lies to Helen about attending an out-of-town conference. He proceeds to vanquish the metal marauder and return to suburbia invigorated. However, a second trip to the island lands him in a trap laid by an old pest with a score to settle: Buddy. Now calling himself Syndrome, it seems this madman inventor, weapons trafficker, and wannabe crusader has been flushing out and eliminating the world's true superheroes one by one.

Back home, Helen smells something fishy. Clues prompt her to contact a brassy little woman named Edna Mode, a German fashion diva who unveils new supersuits for the entire family. That visit helps Helen connect the dots. Feeling concerned and betrayed, she leaps into action and follows a homing beacon to the island to retrieve her husband (with stowaways Violet and Dash aboard). Missiles fly. Machine guns blaze. Syndrome and his henchmen show no mercy. Still, Helen's maternal instinct is strong. Even the bickering sibs learn to cooperate. Indeed, if they're going to succeed, everyone must band together and use their unique abilities to escape the island and foil Syndrome's nefarious plot, which leads them back to Metroville.

Joined by their old friend Frozone, the Parrs battle and eventually subdue Syndrome's mechanical monster as it rampages through the city streets. But Syndrome isn't a gracious loser. He heads straight for their suburban home and threatens to make off with baby Jack-Jack, only to learn the hard way that the little guy has his own unpredictable super-powers. Once again in Metroville's good graces, the Parrs can relax and, within reason, enjoy being themselves. Which is super.

The savvy folks at Pixar have built a reputation for creating warm, humorous, kinetic, and truly intelligent animated films that tell stories of substance. Writer/director Brad Bird loves the studio's amazing computer graphics, but says, "I often think people stress the technology too much. The heart of the matter is still characters."[5] And a well-crafted story. And moral themes. Which is why *The Incredibles* deserves an in-depth look.

Before You Watch

Carve out a half hour to read 1 Corinthians 12 together and list in detail the unique gifts that make each member of your household valuable to the family. Attitudes. Talents. Personality traits. Specific contributions. Write down as many as you can. At some future date—with everyone gathered around—you can share the list aloud as a gift of love and encouragement.

Bible Bookmarks

1 Cor. 9:24 and 12; Ex. 17:8-16; Deut. 28:1; Gen. 4:1-12; Num. 12; 3 Jn. 9-11; Jas. 4:1-12; Prov. 5:15-20, 22:1; Eph. 6:10-18

Talking Points

1. Early on, Mr. Incredible boasts that he prefers to work alone. How does he come to regret that attitude? What does he learn about his family's ability to do more together than any one of

75

them could do alone? Read Exodus 17:8-16 and imagine what would have happened had Moses gone solo and refused help from others.

2. In separate scenes Bob, Dash, and Syndrome all note that calling everyone "special" or "super" simply diminishes those who truly are and encourages mediocrity. What do you think about that? Scriptures such as Deuteronomy 28:1 and 1 Corinthians 9:24 clearly prescribe a path toward excellence.

3. Writer/director Brad Bird has said, "Violet is a typical teenager, someone who's not comfortable in her own skin and is in that rocky place between being a kid and an adult. So invisibility seemed like the right superpower for her."[6] Ask, "Do you agree or disagree? Why? What other superpowers might befit modern teens?"

4. To improve his own image, Syndrome gets rid of the competition by doing away with the true heroes. Do you know people at school or work who would rather tear down others than strive for personal excellence? Biblical examples include Genesis 4:1-12, Numbers 12, and 3 John 9-11 (find the solution in James 4:1-12). Who are the pseudo-heroes in our culture, and who are the real ones they'd like to eliminate?

5. Syndrome bitterly remarks that he only earned Mr. Incredible's respect *after* he became a threat. Sadly, many bullies (at school or in global politics) feel the same way. Talk about that. How can we treat everyone with the kind of respect Jesus demonstrated?

6. Helen tells the kids, "Your identity is your most valuable possession. Protect it." What does she mean? Why is it important? Relate this to Proverbs 22:1.

7. The film has a lot to say about midlife crisis, particularly from a male point of view. Help your teen understand what Edna means by "Men at Robert's age are unstable, prone to weakness." Explain how the full armor of God is a spiritual super-suit designed to protect us at all stages of life (Ephesians 6:10-18).

8. Though Bob never seriously considers being unfaithful to Helen, what aspects of his "innocent flirtation" with Mirage crossed a line? Why? Where would you have drawn it? Examine Solomon's wisdom about fidelity in marriage in Proverbs 5:15-20.

9. Mirage tells Syndrome, "Valuing life is not a weakness, and disregarding it is not strength." Talk about that. How does this truth apply to the battle over the sanctity of human life today?

10. Helen realizes she expected too much of Violet on the plane, and

reassures her that her gifts will develop in time. If you have put undue pressure on your teen to think or behave like an adult, take this opportunity to apologize, point to their strengths, and express confidence in them.

Follow-Up Activity

Creator Brad Bird laid the foundation for his film first by deciding what he considered "heroic" and how to personify that. Take some time to create your own superheroes from scratch, independently. Have them reflect your ideals. Be creative. What are their secret identities and what do they do when they're not fighting crime? Give them specific powers and indicate how they might use them for the greater good. Explain where those abilities came from. Draw or describe them in costume (include capes at your own risk). Do they have archenemies? Sidekicks? Gadgets? Cool vehicles? Let your imaginations run wild for a few days. Then go out for dinner and, while you're waiting for your food, unveil and describe your heroes to each other.

Just for Fun

Near the end of the film we see two elderly men talking about being "old school." They are cartoon renderings of Frank Thomas and Ollie Johnston, surviving members of Walt Disney's team of master animators from the studio's early years. The men, both in their nineties, provided the voices themselves.

—Bob Smithouser

The Lord of the Rings

Rated: PG-13
Themes: Friendship, perseverance, good vs. evil, temptation, addiction, prejudice, stewardship, ecology, heroic sacrifice, providence, romantic love, spiritual warfare, teamwork, servant leadership, embracing a calling, coping with separation and loss, resurrection and redemption
Total Running Time: 9 hours, 17 minutes (Part 1: 2 hrs. 58 min; Part 2: 2 hrs. 59 min; Part 3: 3 hrs. 20 min)
Starring: Elijah Wood as Frodo; Viggo Mortensen as Aragorn; Ian McKellen as Gandalf; Sean Astin as Sam; Liv Tyler as Arwen; Orlando Bloom as Legolas; John Rhys-Davies as Gimli
Directed by: Peter Jackson

The following Movie Nights are based on the theatrical versions of New Line Cinema's three-part epic, not the extended versions which run an extra 2 hours, 4 minutes and contain additional cautions.

Cautions

Despite its moral core, life lessons, and adventurous spirit, *The Lord of the Rings* is not for everyone. At its heart this Oscar-winning phenomenon is a brooding war epic in three acts. The small- and large-scale conflicts grow increasingly dark and violent as the story unfolds, pitting the forces of good against hideous, unrelenting beasts. Evil *looks* evil. Some moments are creepy, others grotesque; still others are menacingly intense. On a spiritual level, while Gandalf and Saruman have been compared to faithful and fallen angels accountable to a higher power,[7] the mere mention of "wizards" or "sorcerers" will give some families pause. Also, characters drink ale and smoke pipes. For

79

more information about specific scenes, examine detailed content breakdowns at pluggedinonline.com.

 ## Story Summary

When J. R. R. Tolkien created Middle-earth and its inhabitants in the early 1950s, the author never could have dreamed that a half-century later the world still would be enamored with hobbits, elves, dwarves, and orcs. Peter Jackson's blockbuster trilogy begins with a brief history lesson explaining the dark lord Sauron's deception of men, and his forging of an evil ring making him all but invincible. Sauron became separated from this diabolical ring, which changed hands several times before finding its way to Bilbo Baggins, a diminutive hobbit living in the pastoral splendor of the Shire.

We join the story as wee Shirefolk celebrate Bilbo's birthday, unaware that Middle-earth stands at a crossroads. Sauron is marshaling sinister forces in preparation for a grand battle meant to destroy the world of men. *And he wants that ring.* Reduced to a fiery, disembodied eye atop a stone tower, the still-dangerous Sauron narrows his search to the Shire and, aided by a traitorous wizard named Saruman, dispatches wraiths on horseback to retrieve his prize. Bilbo's friend, the wise wizard Gandalf, senses trouble and entrusts the ring to Bilbo's innocent nephew Frodo who, accompanied by hobbit pals Sam, Merry, and Pippin, embarks on a perilous journey to the land of the elves where the ring will be safe until a council can decide what to do next. Along the way the hobbits encounter Aragorn (a.k.a. Strider), a cloaked ranger who becomes their protector.

Once the ring arrives in Rivendell, representatives of diverse races and tribes form a fellowship. Their mission: Escort the ring into the heart of enemy territory and destroy it the only way they can—by throwing it into the fiery volcano from whence it came. Gandalf, Aragorn, and the four hobbits are joined by an elf (Legolas), a dwarf (Gimli), and Boromir, a soldier of Gondor who wants to use the ring as a weapon for good. Boromir doesn't understand that it was created *by* evil *for* evil and will only possess and ravage what is good and true.

During the journey the fellowship must travel through the mines of Moria where they battle a tentacled beast, a cave troll, and swarms of hideous orcs before Gandalf bravely stares down a winged behemoth and is overcome. The others do their best to carry on but wind up scattered when Uruk-hai warriors attack. Boromir is killed. Armored beasts make off with Merry and Pippin, requiring that Aragorn, Legolas, and Gimli go after them. The ring-bearer, Frodo, heads toward Mordor accompanied by his most loyal friend, Sam.

Chaos in their captors' camp allows Merry and Pippin to escape into a mysterious forest inhabited by Ents, plodding tree shepherds who consider the looming war someone else's problem until they learn that Saruman has destroyed part of the forest to fuel his war machine. Meanwhile Aragorn, Legolas, and Gimli meet up with a resurrected Gandalf, as well as a legion of horsemen from the troubled nation of Rohan. It seems Saruman and a slimy sidekick have been poisoning the mind of Rohan's good King Theoden. Gandalf liberates Theoden and warns him that his people are in grave danger. The king responds by moving everyone to Helm's Deep, an impenetrable fortress. During the evacuation, Theoden's niece takes a liking to Aragorn, not realizing that his heart belongs to elf princess Arwen who is trying to decide whether to follow her people to the undying lands or trade her immortality for a season as Aragorn's bride. But the love story takes a back seat to the war story. Helm's Deep eventually comes under spectacular attack by an Uruk-hai army of 10,000 until reinforcements drive the enemy hoard back.

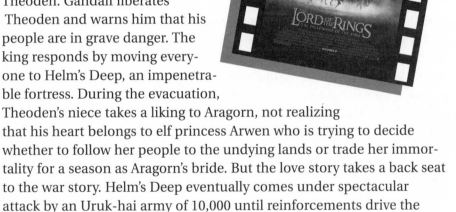

As for Frodo and Sam, they've been stalked by an emaciated creature named Gollum. This former owner of the ring remains addicted to "the precious" and obsessed with getting it back. Sam clearly sees Gollum as a threat, while Frodo takes pity on the creature, convincing it to serve as their guide. The closer the trio get to Mordor, the more Gollum drives a wedge between the two hobbits, and the more Frodo labors beneath the enormous spiritual and emotional weight of the ring. Isolating Frodo from his companion, Gollum lures the ring-bearer into the lair of a giant spider in hopes that it will finish him off. But Sam saves the day.

The ferocious battle at Helm's Deep turns out to be a mere skirmish compared to the conflict brewing outside Minas Tirith. With every dark army in Middle-earth marching toward the capitol city of Gondor, its steward, Denethor, can do nothing but mourn the loss of his favorite son Boromir, whose nobler brother can find no favor in his father's eyes. Amidst all of this family strife, Gandalf takes charge, rallying the city's defenses until they appear overrun. That's when Aragorn (the true king of Gondor who has yet to assume the throne) shows up with an army of the dead and turns the tide. All that remains is for them to preoccupy the forces of darkness long enough to give Frodo time to dispose of the ring. However, just as the ring-bearer stands poised to drop his charge into a river of magma, Frodo suddenly refuses to destroy it. An opportunistic grab by Gollum sends the ring tumbling into the fire. Sauron is defeated, Middle-earth is saved, and Aragorn becomes king with Arwen at his side.

They say it's always darkest before the dawn. That's certainly true of this epic. The side of good suffers losses: loss of life, loss of innocence. Although good triumphs over evil, Tolkien realized that victory comes at a price. As you and your teen explore each of the three films, keep in mind that *The Lord of the Rings* was never intended to be allegorical. It merely uses a dynamic mythology, created from a Christian worldview, to comment on transcendent issues that touch us all.

Before You Watch

In the days or weeks prior to viewing, read through some New Testament passages that examine Jesus' disciples' personalities and backgrounds. Consider how, without a divine prerogative, they might have had a hard time getting along. (For example, Peter was outspoken and inconsistent, while John was quiet but loyal; Matthew had collected taxes for Rome, while Simon the Zealot was militantly anti-establishment.) Ask your teen if there are people in his or her life who are disagreeable or hard to understand because of such differences. Be prepared to revisit this conversation later in light of Gimli's distrust of Legolas, Gandalf's contempt for Pippin, or the prideful Boromir's lack of respect for the true king, Aragorn.

Bible Bookmarks

Part 1—Heb. 12:1-2; Isa. 6:8; 1 Sam. 16:7; 1 Cor. 1:26-29; 2 Chron. 33-34; Matt. 5:7; Prov. 16:18; Jas. 1:13-15 **Part 2**—Jn. 15:13; Matt. 6:24; Prov. 18:24; 2 Cor. 6:14; Zech. 7:8-10; Rom. 7:14-25; Ps. 103:12; Deut. 20:19; 1 Cor. 12:14-20; Ps. 20:7; 44:4-8 **Part 3**—Rom. 5:3-5; Gen. 3:1-5; Rom. 12:3; Lk. 12:35-48; 1 Pet. 2:9; Deut. 18:11; Rev. 21:1-22:6; Gal. 5:1, 6:2; Isa. 40:28-31

The Fellowship of the Ring

Talking Points

1. In the introduction, Galadriel says that Sauron poured "cruelty, malice, and a will to dominate all life" into the one ring that would rule all others. How is Sauron's character like Satan's?

2. Unlike pop-culture wizard Harry Potter, Gandalf is accountable to a higher power and believes in providence. Lines such as "Bilbo was *meant* to find the ring, in which case you also were *meant* to have it, and that is an encouraging thought" imply that a good, divine authority watches over Middle-earth. Why is this important?

3. Read Hebrews 12:1-2. Bilbo gets greedily suspicious when Gandalf asks him for the ring, causing the wizard to remind him who he's dealing with ("I'm not trying to rob you. I'm trying to help you. . . . Trust me as you once did. Let it go."). How can we sometimes react like Bilbo when our wise, loving God tells us to lay aside something pleasurable that could harm us?

4. Consider Frodo's willingness to escort the ring to Mordor in light of Isaiah 6:8. Is God calling you to take a similar leap of faith? What's stopping you? Fortunately, the hobbits didn't focus on their shortcomings. They may not be very big, but they've got it where it counts, much like the servants God values (1 Samuel 16:7, 1 Corinthians 1:26-29).

5. Gimli's faith lies in his axe. During the council, he attempts to destroy the ring with it and the axe shatters. How does this illustrate our need to attack spiritual problems with spiritual weapons, not our own strength or wisdom?

6. Aragorn fears he may not have the character to overcome the weakness his bloodline has shown in the past. Sins *can* be passed down

through generations, but they can also be reversed. Read 2 Chronicles 33-34 to see how Judah's King Josiah undid the evil practiced by the two generations of leaders before him.

7. In the mines of Moria, Gandalf warns Frodo, "Do not be too eager to deal out death and judgment," noting that pity and mercy are virtues that can yield fruit. How does this echo Jesus' words in Matthew 5:7? How does it relate to you?

8. Beginning to feel the weight of his burden, Frodo expresses regret that he must bear it. Talk about Gandalf's response, "So do all who live to see such times, but that is not for them to decide. All we have to decide is what to do with the time that is given to us." What burden do you carry that you wish you didn't have to bear? How will you redeem the time given to you?

9. Staring down the Balrog, Gandalf insists, "You shall not pass!" Is some moral challenge demanding that you take that kind of stand? Will you do it? How?

10. The loss of Gandalf throws the fellowship into mourning and some self-doubt, feeling unable to continue without their mentor and guide. Have you experienced a similar loss? When? How did you find the strength to go on?

11. Although Galadriel doesn't accept the ring from Frodo, she fantasizes about the benefits of doing so. Why is it dangerous to let our minds wander that way?

12. Read Proverbs 16:18. How did Boromir's pride, frustration, and misunderstanding of the mission lead to his downfall? In what ways is he like Judas in the Gospels? How is he different? How does Boromir's story reflect James 1:13-15?

13. Well-intentioned characters hoped to use the ring—created for evil—as a tool for good. It proved their undoing. What are some ways people fall prey to similar temptations? (Example: lying for a noble cause)

The Two Towers

Talking Points

1. Compare Gandalf's stand against the Balrog to Jesus' supreme confrontation with death and hell itself (John

15:13). How are their subsequent resurrections similar? Different?

2. When characters introduce themselves, they include the names of their fathers. Why is this important to them? How might our society be stronger if more individuals valued ties to stock and stories bigger than their own?

3. Actor Andy Serkis says he played Gollum as a 60-year-old heroin addict. In what ways does Gollum's obsession with the ring compare to other forms of addiction? How does Gollum's attempt to serve both "the precious" and Frodo reflect Matthew 6:24?

4. Grima was poisoning King Theoden's mind, impeding his judgment. How can Satan's whispers do the same to us? Note: Grima didn't convince Theoden to switch sides; he simply distorted the truth to make him ineffective, which can be the greater danger to Christ followers.

5. The Bible is full of friendships that prove Proverbs 18:24. David and Jonathan. Naomi and Ruth. Examine the deep bond shared by Frodo and Sam and how it has been put to the test. Odds are teens have had a wedge driven into a relationship by a third party or difficult circumstance. Invite them to talk about it.

6. In 2 Corinthians 6:14, we are warned to be careful about the alliances we form. Yet Zechariah 7:8-10 and other scriptures preach compassion, forgiveness, and mercy. In the debate over Gollum, which verse might Frodo use to state his case? How about Sam? Why would each have a valid argument? And why is Frodo so desperate to believe that Gollum can be saved?

7. How does the inner turmoil between Smeagol and Gollum represent the spiritual battle with our flesh described in Romans 7:14-25? In the midst of that conflict, the creature's dark side dredges up past crimes in an attempt to define and control its rival. Psalm 103:12 comes in handy when Satan tries to do the same to us.

8. Despite his daughter's wishes to live a mortal life as Aragorn's mate, Elrond sends Arwen off toward the Grey Havens "for her own good." Was he right to do so? Why or why not?

9. How did Saruman's clearing of the forest to fuel "the fires of industry" violate a biblical principal found in Deuteronomy 20:19? What would you consider to be a healthy balance between progress and ecology? Ask, "What can our family do to be better stewards of the environment?"

10. Eowyn is a fighter who struggles with the social expectations of her as a woman. Is there more than one way to achieve the "valor" she desires? Read 1 Corinthians 12:14-20. Ask your teen, "Have you ever felt underappreciated and forced into a role? How?"

11. King Theoden has put his faith in the reliable walls of Helm's Deep during times of crisis. Ask, "What is *your* Helm's Deep, that thing you trust to protect you when all else fails?" (Assuming the answer is God, probe a little to find out what comes in second. Grades? Family? Friends? Financial security? A job?) Read Psalm 20:7 and 44:4-8.

12. British statesman Edmund Burke said, "All that is necessary for the triumph of evil is that good men do nothing." How does this truth apply to the Ents? What finally got Treebeard's attention?

13. Weak and confused in Osgiliath, Frodo is drawn toward the Nazgul until his clear-thinking friend Sam pulls him away. Similarly, Theoden needs Gandalf to snap him out of his funk. How can the Lord rescue us that way when things are cloudy and we're tempted to give ourselves over to darkness (e.g., clarity of Scripture, wise counsel)?

The Return of the King

Talking Points

1. Revisit the "Before You Watch" activity and talk about how early strife between certain members of the fellowship changed over time. What were some pivotal moments? Consider how a divine calling and a common goal can unite extremely different people.

2. How does Romans 5:3-5 apply to the changes witnessed in various characters during the journey? In the end, who did you admire most? Why?

3. It's been said of parenting, "Rules without relationship lead to rebellion." Relate this to Pippin defying Gandalf to sneak a second look at the seeing stone. (Gandalf deprived him of it earlier without adequately explaining the danger, so the hobbit took a forbidden peek with near-tragic results.) How could each have behaved better? What are the lessons for your family?

4. Gollum turns Frodo against Sam by causing him to doubt his faithful friend's motives and character. Read Genesis 3:1-5. How did

Satan use the same tactic on Eve? How does Gollum's final act make others' mercy toward him pay off?

5. Denethor forgets he is merely minding the store in Gondor, inspiring Gandalf to scold, "Authority is not given to you to deny the return of the king, steward!" Read Romans 12:3 and Jesus' parable in Luke 12:35-48. Which steward is like Denethor? What does that parable have to say to us?

6. Weigh Denethor and Faramir's family crisis. How does this tension illustrate a son's need for his father's love and approval? Do you think this is as big an issue for mothers and daughters? Why or why not? How did Denethor's favoritism toward Boromir aggravate things?

7. Arwen defies her father and stays behind with Aragorn. Is she justified? Why? Her final decision isn't based solely on romantic love, but *maternal* love. She realizes that her son will never experience life if she acts selfishly. How might understanding Arwen's vision and values help a pregnant teen resist having an abortion?

8. "Put aside the ranger. Become who you were born to be." Consider Elrond's words to Aragorn and their similarity to a reminder given to God's people that they are special and set apart (1 Peter 2:9). How, then, should we live?

9. Since Deuteronomy 18:11 says it's detestable to "consult with the dead," how do you feel about the heroes recruiting an army of the dead to fight on the side of good? Why?

10. When the battle for Gondor appears lost, Gandalf reassures Pippin, "The journey doesn't end here. Death is just another path, one that we all must take." He confidently describes a glorious afterlife. Share John's glimpse of heaven in Revelation 21:1-22:6.

11. Near Mount Doom Sam sees how the ring has exhausted Frodo. Sam tells him, "I can't carry it for you, but I can carry you!" Galatians 6:2 instructs us to bear one another's burdens. Think of someone with a burden that you simply cannot carry. How might you, like Sam, "carry *your friend*"? Draw strength from Isaiah 40:28-31.

12. When Frodo reaches the fiery precipice and puts the ring on, we think, *Noooo! You can't come this far only to surrender to selfishness!* What are some similar ways people make poor choices today and fail to finish strong?

13. Imagine being among those freed from Sauron's grip as the tower falls and the enemy is crushed. Can you picture Aragorn or Legolas, in

the wake of such a victory, walking into Mordor and turning himself over to the enemy remnant? Ridiculous, right? Yet in spite of Christ's spectacular victory over sin, those He freed can willingly choose captivity to sin. Read Galatians 5:1 and determine to live like one set free.

Follow-Up Activity

Go to "Appendix I" in the back of this book. The cast was asked, "While working on these movies, did you learn a particular life lesson that would be valuable for teens today?" Talk about the stars' responses. Do you agree or disagree with their comments? Why? What spiritual insights might make the advice even more meaningful?

For further reflection on J. R. R. Tolkien's masterpiece from a biblical perspective, pick up a copy of the book *Finding God in The Lord of the Rings* by Kurt Bruner and Jim Ware.

Just for Fun

Theatrically, this trilogy grossed more than a billion dollars in the U.S. It also earned Best Picture nominations for each of the three films, and took home a record-tying 11 Oscars for *Return of the King*. That should be some consolation for Viggo Mortensen, whose body took a real beating during filming. In addition to having a front tooth snapped off while shooting the hand-to-hand conflict at Helm's Deep, he nearly drowned after being swept away by a river (the scene where he's rescued by his horse). Also, when he kicks the helmet in grief, that scream is real. Viggo broke two toes, yet kept acting.

—*Bob Smithouser*

A Man for All Seasons

Rated: G
Themes: Religious faith, integrity, courage of convictions, persecution, compromise, temptation, betrayal, martyrdom, tyranny over speech, importance of an oath
Running Time: 2 hours
Starring: Paul Scofield as Sir Thomas More; Robert Shaw as King Henry VIII; Orson Welles as Cardinal Wolsey; John Hurt as Richard Rich; Leo McKern as Thomas Cromwell
Directed by: Fred Zinnemann

Cautions

By today's standards, this film qualifies as PG. Its half-dozen or so profanities include a surprised man uttering "Jesus," as well as two uses of g—d—. Sir Thomas More is beheaded just out of frame.

Story Summary

Based on Robert Bolt's play and honored with six Oscars including Best Director, Best Actor (Scofield), and Best Picture of 1966, *A Man for All Seasons* relates the historical struggle over principle between haughty King Henry VIII of England and virtuous Sir Thomas More. That moral impasse led to More's martyrdom in 1535. Teens mature enough to handle some archaic language and old-school cinematic technique (more pleasing in the widescreen format) will be rewarded with a portrait of Christian integrity they won't soon forget.

We learn that Sir Thomas More, a lawyer by trade, has been presiding over civil disputes as a member of Henry's high council. The only thing

More values above public service and intellectual sparring is his unwavering faith in Christ. He is a man of conscience, prayer, and orthodoxy. Perhaps that's why he's a respected liaison between the king and the Catholic Church. But More would rather do what's right than climb social or political ladders. So when Henry announces that he will divorce the barren Katherine of Aragon and wed Anne Boleyn to produce an heir, More refuses to rubber-stamp the union.

The wishy-washy Cardinal Wolsey is afraid of upsetting the king. He urges More to reconsider, chiding him for viewing facts with a "horrible moral squint." More counters, "When statesmen forsake their own private conscience for the sake of their public duties, they lead their country by a short route to chaos." He doesn't publicly denounce the king (a serious offense), but cleverly resists registering any opinion, even to friends and family who know his heart.

In one scene, More is swarmed by commoners hoping to gain favor in court. One gives him a silver goblet. Upon realizing it was meant as a bribe, More passes the cup to an ambitious young man named Richard Rich who keeps pestering More to hire him. He warns the flawed Rich that judges must be immune to ethical temptations, and advises him to seek employment elsewhere. Rich doesn't handle rejection well. He soon wanders into a political den of vipers bent on bringing More down.

Nevertheless, King Henry respects More. He promises to spare him trouble provided he doesn't vocally oppose the divorce from Katherine. But More's silence starts rumors. Word spreads that this paragon of virtue—now Chancellor of England—disapproves. The higher More's post, the more conspicuous is his failure to endorse the king's divorce. The heat rises again when archbishops are strong-armed into renouncing the Pope's authority and declaring Henry "supreme head of the church in England." Such arrogance and hostility inspires Sir Thomas to resign.

After the royal wedding, administrator Thomas Cromwell launches a malicious campaign (based on scurrilous reports by Rich and others) to force a definitive statement from More. A law concocted for this purpose insists that all citizens either take an oath recognizing Anne as Queen, or stand guilty of high treason. By refusing to go on record, More earns himself prison time in the Tower of London. During a rare visit from his family, his daughter appeals to him:

Margaret: Father, God more regards the thoughts of the heart than the words of the mouth, or so you've always told me.

More: Yes.

Margaret: Then say the words of the oath and in your heart think otherwise.

More: What is an oath then, but words we say to God? When a man takes an oath he is holding his own self in his hands like water, and if he opens his fingers, then he needn't hope to find himself again.

His moorings are deep, his faith strong. In one final appearance before Parliament, this courageous saint faces a kangaroo court that sentences him to death by beheading.

Before You Watch

The more teens know about the historical figures, events, and political climate portrayed in the film, the easier it will be for them to follow the story. A good place to start is helpful online biographies found at www.luminarium.org/renlit/morebio.htm and www.infoplease.com/ce6/people/A0858608.html.

Bible Bookmarks

Matt. 5:10-16, 26:57-66; Lev. 18:16; 1 Ki. 22:1-28; Jn. 15:18-21; Dan. 3; Heb. 11:35b-40; Prov. 28:13-14

Talking Points

1. Was More too stubborn or did he do the right thing? After frustrating the king he tells his wife, "I couldn't find the other way." In the end, *was* there another way? Compare More's interrogation and trial to what Jesus faced before the Sanhedrin (Matthew 26:57-66).

2.   Rich doesn't like the idea of becoming a teacher because it won't bring him glory. More points out that he would have the respect of himself, his pupils, his friends, and God ("Not a bad public, there"). Why should that be enough in any profession? Why *isn't* it for many people? Also, discuss More's advice, "A man should go where he won't be tempted."

3.   After Rich first betrays More, Cromwell assures him, "You'll find it easier next time." How can we harden our hearts to the Holy Spirit the more we commit the same sin? Why does that happen? Why is true repentance so important? Read Proverbs 28:13-14.

4.   With historical hindsight, discuss the philosophical rift between More and Will over the Protestant Reformation.

5.   Henry invokes Leviticus 18:16 to support his immoral agenda. But confronted with scripture that *weakens* his case, he argues, "Deuteronomy is ambiguous" and blames God for creating his situation in the first place. In what ways do people do that today?

6.   Read the story of Ahab and Jehoshaphat in 1 Kings 22:1-28. How does Henry's desire for More's approval compare to the king's desire for the prophet's blessing? What about Micaiah's and More's reputations made their opinions matter? How can our integrity be, as Jesus illustrated in Matthew 5:10-16, "salt and light" to our world?

7.   The witch hunt against More should help us appreciate our freedom of speech and why America's forefathers felt the need to fight for it. How has the First Amendment been abused in recent years?

8.   Talk about More's statement, "If we lived in a state where virtue was profitable, common sense would make us saintly. But since we see that avarice, anger, pride, and stupidity commonly profit far beyond charity, modesty, justice, and thought, perhaps we must stand fast a little, even at the risk of being heroes." How does this relate to your world?

9.   Facing death, Cardinal Wolsey expresses regrets over misplaced loyalties. More does not. How did each man's priorities in life impact his sense of self at the end of life? How can you live with no regrets?

10. Except for More, it seemed every man had a price "for his soul." What were some of them?

11. Western culture has become increasingly hostile to "intolerant" Christians who believe in exclusive, absolute truth. Is there a line you won't cross? Have you faced persecution for that righteous stand?

Follow-Up Activity

Take a few days to let the movie sink in. Then schedule 30 minutes to share this short devotion:

1) Begin with thoughts or feelings you've had about the film since your Movie Night.

2) Read Daniel 3. Note that, just as More's willingness to die for his religious beliefs has emboldened the saints for nearly 500 years, Christians have also been encouraged by Shadrach, Meshach, and Abednego, who faced execution for not bowing to a king's idol.

3) While all refused to compromise, More's fate was different from that trio's. Talk about that, and how God makes no guarantees that by doing what's right we'll avoid persecution or even death.

4) Refer to Jesus' words in John 15:18-21 and read Hebrews 11:35b-40 for biblical examples of martyrdom. (You may also want to reference *Fox's Book of Martyrs* to learn about other heroes of the faith.)

5) Finally, pray with your teen that both of you would have the wisdom to know the truth—and the strength to stand up for it—whatever the future holds.

Just for Fun

Fred Zinnemann also directed *Oklahoma!, High Noon,* and *From Here to Eternity.* Two of his actors in this film later became famous for characters now embedded in the pop-culture consciousness. Robert Shaw starred as the obsessed Captain Quint in Steven Spielberg's *Jaws.* John Hurt played Kane, the doomed crewman in *Alien* renowned for having a space creature burst out of his chest.

—Bob Smithouser

The Man Who Shot Liberty Valance

Rated: Not Rated
Themes: Brute force vs. civil justice, responding to bullies, courage, sobriety, journalistic ethics, settling the West, myth vs. reality, honor, the importance of education
Running Time: 2 hours, 3 minutes
Starring: John Wayne as Tom Doniphon; James Stewart as Ransom Stoddard; Vera Miles as Hallie Stoddard; Lee Marvin as Liberty Valance; Edmond O'Brien as Dutton Peabody; Andy Devine as Marshal Link Appleyard
Directed by: John Ford

Cautions

Like most old westerns, this one contains a lot of tobacco and alcohol use. Lawless violence includes beatings, whippings, vandalism, and a fatal gunfight.

Story Summary

Having traversed a barren landscape of mesas, scrub brush, and tumbleweeds, a locomotive pulls into the sleepy town of Shinbone carrying a famous senator and his wife. It's a grim homecoming for Ransom and Hallie Stoddard. They're there for a burial. Most locals don't know anyone has died, much less someone important enough to merit a visit from Senator Stoddard. When a curious newspaper editor insists the mourners tell him the story behind the fellow in the pine box, Stoddard relates his history with rugged cowboy Tom Doniphon.

It begins as "Ranse" Stoddard, an idealistic young lawyer, heads west. A gang led by notorious scoundrel Liberty Valance robs the stage and roughs up Ranse, who learns the hard way that due process isn't the most efficient form of justice in the yet-untamed West. Left for dead, he's rescued by Tom who, along with the proprietors of a local diner (including the lovely Hallie), clean him up and warn him that going after Valance will require a gun. Ranse doesn't believe in violence. "I know those law books mean a lot to you, but not out here," says Tom, the one man in town tougher than Valance, "Out here a man settles his own problems."

Although he can't expect help from Shinbone's spineless marshal, Ranse intends to see law and order rule—and Valance behind bars. A second encounter with the bully finds Tom stepping in, only to have Ranse end the standoff with a tirade about civility. But he's more than noble talk. Ranse starts teaching school and gives the locals civics lessons. He helps Mr. Peabody write for the local newspaper, which adopts the righteous but dangerous stand of siding with homesteaders against lawless cattlemen opposed to statehood.

A public election to nominate delegates gets interrupted by Valance. More than just a troublemaker, he's also a hired gun paid by big ranchers to intimidate the locals. Denied a nomination, Liberty challenges Ranse to a gunfight. Tom and others urge Ranse to leave town. But after Liberty and his boys ambush Peabody and beat him half to death, Ranse accepts the challenge. Liberty toys with the inept gunman before going in for the kill. Shots ring out. The desperado falls dead. As Hallie nurses Ranse's wounds, Tom shows up jealous and ready to drown his pain. A failure at romance, the drunken, despairing Tom sets his own house ablaze.

Soon the entire territory gathers to decide who it will send to Washington.

Peabody waxes eloquently on Ranse's behalf, though the peaceable lawyer struggles with the fact that much of his acclaim comes from gunning a man down. But who *was* the man who shot Liberty Valance? Tom takes Ranse aside and confidentially tells him *he* did it from a nearby alley. He did it for Hallie ("She wanted you alive. . . . Hallie's your girl now"). He orders Ranse to accept the nomination and make her proud.

This film is about people, but more importantly, it memorializes old-fashioned cowboy masculinity riding off into the sunset—and dying in obscurity—while being replaced by the noble Everyman. The balance of power in the Old West has shifted. The gunslinger is out; the politician is in. And Hallie is emblematic of the West itself, a prize to be won by the ideal left standing. She desires frontier toughness *and* civilized evolution. Since she can't have both she chooses to move forward, but with a romantic longing. When the elderly Ranse returns to Shinbone, the town, changed forever by progress, is briefly reminded of its own myth and legend, which the newspaper editor decides is worth protecting.

Before You Watch

The film extols the benefits of America being a republic, a system in which citizens can change things by appointing worthy delegates and voting. Prime the pump. Casually ask your teen how they feel about our system of government and what issues will be most important to them when they start voting.

Bible Bookmarks

Lk. 6:27-36, 10:25-37; Prov. 20:1; 1 Thess. 5:15; Matt. 15:19, 16:24; Ps. 119:97-104; Gal. 5:13-26; Mk. 1:16-20; Isa. 6:8; Eph. 5:18

Talking Points

1. How does Tom's rescue of Ranse early in the film compare with Jesus' parable of the "Good Samaritan" (Luke 10:25-37)? Imagine a modern scenario in which God might ask you to do likewise.

2. Hallie's main motivation for learning to read is access to the Bible ("I know the Good Book from preacher talk, but it'd be a soul

97

comfort if I could read the words myself."). It's easy to take for granted our easy access to Scripture. Read Psalm 119:97-104 and try to catch David's vision. Could you be spending more time in God's Word?

3. On a scale of 1 to 10, how well did Ranse handle Liberty's bullying? What things did he do (or not do) that caused you to rate him that way? Read 1 Thessalonians 5:15 and Luke 6:27-36. At what point is it appropriate for a victim to defend himself?

4. In spite of all of Ranse's accomplishments, the reason the man on the train gushes over him is because he killed Liberty. What did that say to Ranse, and how do you think it made him feel? Also, what does Hallie's gesture of putting the cactus rose on Tom's coffin tell Ranse?

5. The blackboard in Ranse's class reads, "Education is the basis of law and order." Do you agree it's that simple? Does this account for man's fallen nature (Matthew 15:19)? Find the simple formula for law and order in Galatians 5:13-26.

6. Why is the marshal a pivotal figure? Consider the following statement: *Laws only work if they are a natural deterrent and if someone is willing to enforce them.* How does this apply to society, as well as in the supernatural realm?

7. Despite having strong feelings about the need for statehood, Tom and Peabody don't want to be delegates. Tom sees it as an interruption of his personal plans. The newspaperman is more comfortable writing about politicians than being one. If a cause is truly important to us, how far should we be willing to go? How does this relate to following Christ (Isaiah 6:8, Mark 1:16-20, Matthew 16:24)? How did Tom sacrificially "give all" in another sense?

8. Drunkenness is portrayed as humorous (Peabody's exploits) and destructive (Tom torching his house). What has our society learned about the effects of alcohol? Has that issue touched your family? Ask your teen what hedges they have constructed related to drinking, and how they would handle certain situations. Read Proverbs 20:1 and Ephesians 5:18.

9. What does the editor mean when he concludes, "When the legend becomes fact, print the legend"? What did that say about his culture's need for heroes and hope? If the media learned about a story like that today, would they try to protect the celebrity's reputation or be the first to expose him? Why? Can you think of examples? What does that say about our culture? Are we more interested in facts or legends?

10. Ask your teen, "In your own words, what is a catch phrase?" Ask them to share one that's popular right now, what it means, and why it's significant. Point out that this film introduced one of John Wayne's trademark expressions ("pilgrim") in the days before movies intentionally tried to create catch phrases.

Follow-Up Activity

Now that your teen has seen John Wayne in action, they might want to learn more about this Hollywood hero and how he earned his legendary status as America's post-WWII symbol of strength, bravery, and patriotism. There's no shortage of Internet sites dedicated to Wayne. Or you could check your local library for a copy of *John Wayne . . . There Rode a Legend,* a fascinating coffee-table book full of photos and insight into the man behind the myth.

Just for Fun

Before his showdown with Ranse, Liberty wins at poker with two pair—aces and eights. That's Ford's way of foreshadowing the outlaw's demise. Known as the "dead man's hand," those same cards were held by Wild Bill Hickok when he was shot in Nuttal and Mann's saloon on August 2, 1876. To this day, superstitious poker players will fold if they receive aces and eights.

—Bob Smithouser

My Dog Skip

Rated: PG
Themes: Friendship, bullying, responsibility, patriotism, segregation, casualties of war, loyalty, taking emotional risks, forgiveness, cowardice
Running Time: 1 hour, 35 minutes
Starring: Frankie Muniz as Willie Morris; Diane Lane as Ellen Morris; Kevin Bacon as Jack Morris; Luke Wilson as Dink Jenkins
Directed by: Jay Russell

Cautions

A dozen mild profanities ("h—," "d—n") or crude expressions ("t-tty baby," "peed his pants"), often from children. Some cruel bullying. Several scenes involve alcohol.

Story Summary

Reflecting on his youth, a man recalls carefree days as a nine-year-old boy growing up in sleepy Yazoo, Mississippi. As Hitler threatened Europe, young Willie Morris had his own bullies to deal with, hills to storm, and lessons to learn. The turning point in his life would be the arrival of a four-legged friend, a feisty Jack Russell terrier named Skip.

The year is 1942. Willie is a meek little guy who relates better to books than to his peers. He's the only child of a cheerful, spontaneous mother and a stern, silently bitter father who lost his leg in battle. Picked on by schoolyard thugs and overlooked by just about everyone else, Willie is fortunate to be the neighbor and pal of Yazoo's local hero, star athlete Dink Jenkins. But when Dink heads off to war, Willie feels abandoned.

Willie's mom thinks he needs a dog, but Dad says no. He worries that a pet is "a heartache waiting to happen." Ellen defies her husband and surprises their son with a terrier pup for his ninth birthday. After spirited debate, Jack agrees to let Skip stay. Good choice. Skip becomes a real dog-about-town, making friends with everyone from the local butcher to the cutest girl in school, Rivers Applewhite. Since any friend of Skip's is a friend of theirs, Willie's social circle expands. That includes connecting with an African American boy from the other side of their segregated town.

The toughest ones to win over are the abusive bullies who tease Willie and take his things, but Skip helps him earn their respect. So the rough-and-tumble trio decides to test Willie with a dare. They tell him the local legend of a vengeful witch, then leave him to spend a night sitting on her grave. That ol' witch doesn't show up, but some nasty moonshiners *do*, and threaten Willie into keeping mum.

As summer wears on, Willie and Rivers share books and discover the innocent blushes of first love. At the movies they see newsreel footage of dogs training for war and decide that Skip should serve his country. They put him through doggy boot camp, only to get turned down by a recruiter. Willie's dejection is merely an emotional appetizer to the smorgasbord of grown-up emotions he'll soon encounter.

Rumor has it Dink is coming home. But when his fans turn out to welcome him, he's not on the bus. Branded a coward for fleeing the front lines, he sneaks home in a cab and drowns his shame in alcohol. Suddenly Yazoo's favorite son is the object of ridicule. Although Willie still has faith in Dink (more than Dink has in himself), it creates tension, especially when Dink fails to show up at Willie's little league game. Willie's pent-up frustration causes him to strike Skip in anger, an uncharacteristically mean act that costs him people's respect, including Rivers's. Skip runs off. He stays missing for a long time. Wracked with guilt, Willie searches frantically for his canine companion, unaware that Skip is trapped in the moonshiners' secret vault. Willie arrives just in time to see one of the men hit Skip with a shovel before Dink comes to his rescue. It's touch and go at the vet's office. For a while it looks like Willie might lose his best friend, though he recalls as an adult, "That day, I became a young man."

My Dog Skip was praised by critics including Richard Roeper (TV's *Ebert & Roeper*) who credited it with being "more surprising and complex than you'd expect from a movie like this." He's right. It's a cut above the typical boy-and-his-dog story, combining multifaceted themes, smart writing, and an excellent cast.

 ## Before You Watch

Since *My Dog Skip* tells a coming-of-age story about events that signify a child's transition into adolescence, ask teens if they can remember a season of life or specific experiences that made them realize they weren't a little kid anymore. Then tell them about turning points *you* witnessed in their lives that impressed upon you that they were growing up. Don't be surprised if your answers are different!

Bible Bookmarks

Prov. 16:32, 17:17; Matt. 5:38-48; Eph. 5:18, 5:22-24, 6:4; Ex. 2:11-14; Col. 3:9-11

Talking Points

1. Discuss the different parenting philosophies of Jack (protective/strict) and Ellen (more liberal/carefree), and why each felt they were right. Ask teens what they believe is an appropriate balance.

2. Which was worse, Ellen defying Jack and buying the dog for Willie, or Jack taking the dog away on the spot? Consider Ephesians 5:22-24 and 6:4.

3. Most teens have either experienced or witnessed bullying first-hand. Ask how it felt to see Willie abused by the tough kids. What should *we* do when someone harasses us? Why do you think Jesus says what he does in Matthew 5:38-48?

103

4. Willie's frustration leads him to lash out at Skip, much to the chagrin of the people at the game. Ask, "Has witnessing a momentary lack of self-control ever caused you to lose respect for someone? Talk about that." Then: "Have *you* ever had a lapse that helps you identify with Willie?" Read about Moses' violent outburst in Exodus 2:11-14 and what the Bible says about controlling our temper (Proverbs 16:32).

5. What in Jack's life might have contributed to his desire to keep his son from dealing with heartache too soon? What experiences (farewell to Dink, seeing the deer killed, searching for lost dog, etc.) prepared Willie to stand alone beside Skip in his darkest hour? How?

6. As an adult, Willie reflects on racial segregation in the south and notes that Skip's inability to see color proved he was much smarter than people. Get your teen's impression of race relations in *their* world. Point to the equality we all enjoy in Christ (Colossians 3:9-11).

7. Along those lines, Willie's dad says, "Folks like to keep things small, Dink. Put you into one pocket or the other. Give a man a label and you never really need to get to know him." What does he mean?

8. What do you think of Dink's decision to run from battle, and of his reasoning, "It ain't the dyin' that's scary, boy. It's the killin'"? Why was it unwise to numb his pain with alcohol? Read Ephesians 5:18.

9. Yazoo, Mississippi, during WWII probably seems like a totally different world to today's teens. In a lot of ways it is. Ask, "Based on what you saw in the film, how is life different today for better or for worse?" Talk specifically about Willie and Rivers's sweet romance, and how kids growing up in a sexualized culture miss out on that kind of innocence.

10. Dink rebounded from despair because he knew someone believed in him. Read Proverbs 17:17 and discuss how it applies to the fact that his friendship with Willie was based on more than his local celebrity.

Follow-Up Activity

Willie's classmate was free to read the Bible in school during show and tell. It was a brief moment, but a telling one. A lot has changed since the 1940s. Help your teen understand the systematic attempt to remove Scripture, God, and prayer from public schools. Research Supreme Court decisions together (starting with 1962's landmark

Engel v. Vitale). It's hypocritical that the "tolerance" valued so highly these days doesn't include a tolerance of Christian faith in public discourse. Secularists would like to bully Christians into silence. Visit the American Center for Law and Justice online at aclj.org for a better understanding of both student *and* workplace rights in this area.

If watching Willie struggle in the outfield had you wishing you could shout encouragement to him, do the next best thing. Take your teen to a little league baseball game and focus on blessing kids who make mistakes. Offer loud, confident words of reassurance. A simple "That's okay, buddy, you'll get 'em next time!" can lift the spirits of a nine-year-old *and* help a teen discover the joy in encouraging strangers.

Just for Fun

The dog playing the part of old Skip at the end of the movie is Moose, the same canine actor who appeared as Eddie on NBC's long-running sitcom *Frasier*. The rest of the time, Skip is played by Moose's son, Enzo. Hmmm. Talented pedigree or Hollywood nepotism?

—Bob Smithouser

105

Rocky

Rated: PG
Themes: Respect, battling great odds, romantic love, unfulfilled dreams, self-discipline, finding value in others, forgiveness, self-control, balancing toughness and compassion
Running Time: 1 hour, 59 minutes
Starring: Sylvester Stallone as Rocky Balboa; Talia Shire as Adrian; Burt Young as Paulie; Carl Weathers as Apollo Creed; Burgess Meredith as Mickey
Directed by: John G. Avildsen

Cautions

This 1976 Best Picture winner contains disrespectful exchanges, several crass sexual expressions ("screw you," "ballin'") and about 20 profanities, including an s-word and four uses of "g—d—." The worst of those problems can be avoided by watching the edited-for-TV version. There's boxing violence, as well as tobacco and alcohol use. Paulie goes on an abusive tear that, while unsettling, exposes the ugly side of drunkenness. Rocky and Adrian kiss passionately. A few asides imply that the couple may have had sex.

Story Summary

If enough people call you a bum, you might start believing it. That's the dilemma facing Rocky Balboa, a streetwise Philadelphia club boxer tired of getting his brains scrambled for a few bucks a night. But that's all he has to lean on. Rocky isn't well educated, and he's too merciful to excel at his day job of collecting for a loan shark who scolds, "How come you didn't break this guy's thumb like I told you to?" It's because, despite being a pugilist, Rocky is a decent, forgiving lug.

Rocky's family consists of a goldfish and two turtles. They provide an excuse to frequent the local pet shop where he cracks bad jokes for a mousy employee named Adrian. She's a shy, insecure woman misunderstood and mistreated by people close to her, including her uncouth, hot-tempered brother, Paulie. But Rocky sees beauty there. He gently pursues her, knowing all too well how it feels to be labeled a loser.

Professionally, Rocky has been held back by the fact that he's a southpaw (which intimidates prospective opponents), and because he lacks the drive and confidence of other fighters. He's hurt when Mickey, the crusty old manager of his neighborhood gym, gives his locker to a younger, more promising protégé. Rocky resists the temptation to be bitter. Rather, he absorbs the blow and moves on, unaware that his fortunes are about to improve. The reigning heavyweight champion, Apollo Creed, learns that an injury will sideline his opponent for a high-profile bicentennial bout. He needs a challenger. With top contenders unavailable on such short notice, the enterprising showman decides to give a local unknown a shot at the title. Balboa isn't sure he should accept, but he gets talked into this once-in-a-lifetime opportunity.

Meanwhile, Rocky and Adrian are developing a sweet friendship. He makes her feel pretty and treats her with respect, causing her to inch out of her shell. She argues that he's *not* a dumb, untalented thug, and she believes he can actually beat Apollo. But before squaring off against the champ, Rocky must battle back feelings of betrayal when Mickey appears on his doorstep wanting to manage him. The old man tries to talk his way back into the good graces of a "son" he abandoned. After responding with stony silence, then a verbal tirade, Rocky extends forgiveness and reconciliation.

Soon Rocky finds himself consumed with a no-frills training regimen.

Cold early-morning runs. Grueling workouts with Mickey. Trips to a meat locker where slabs of meat double as punching bags. In the process, this torchbearer for the American dream gets thrust into the spotlight—a place Paulie would love to join him. But Paulie does more to embarrass Rocky than help him. Feeling unappreciated, Paulie turns to the bottle and becomes abusive. He hurls insults at Adrian and takes a baseball bat to their living room. Adrian boldly puts her brother in his place and asks Rocky if she can stay with him (where they are shown sleeping in separate beds).

The big day approaches. Rocky realizes he's out of his league. All he wants to do is go the distance—something no one has ever done with Apollo—and prove he's not just another bum from the streets. In the ring the showy Creed gets more than he bargained for. A thrilling display goes the full 15 rounds before the champ retains his title in a split decision. Rocky's moral victory is complete when his true prize, Adrian, rushes to his side.

Before You Watch

If your teen likes to watch boxing on TV, settle in some evening and enjoy a match. Let it be the preliminary, under-card bout that primes you for Hollywood's main event.

The character of Rocky Balboa was inspired by New Jersey club fighter Chuck Wepner (nicknamed the "Bayonne Bleeder"), who challenged heavyweight champ Muhammad Ali to a title fight in 1975. Go online together and learn a little about the boxer. As you watch *Rocky*, identify aspects of the film that are similar to what you read.

Bible Bookmarks

1 Cor. 9:24-27, 15:33; 2 Cor. 12:9-10; 2 Tim. 1:7; Prov. 12:26, 16:18, 20:3; Phil. 3:13-14; Heb. 12:1; Mk. 8:34; Joel 2:23-27

Talking Points

1. While skating, Rocky and Adrian allude to how parents' remarks about their flaws affected their self-image and direction in life. Why do the opinions of certain people leave such a

109

mark? Take comfort in the knowledge that everyone has weaknesses and the Lord wants to compensate for them (2 Corinthians 12:9-10).

2. Rocky points out that Adrian is shy by nature. Imagine a "shyness scale" with Adrian as a 10 and the bombastic Apollo as a 1. Where would you fall? Why did you rate yourself that way? How can 2 Timothy 1:7 apply to people who are naturally shy?

3. At Rocky's place following their first date, Adrian says, "I don't know you well enough. I've never been in a man's apartment alone. . . . I'm not comfortable. I should go." How should Rocky have responded? Why?

4. Rocky tries to rescue young Marie from the "yo-yos" on the street corner by explaining that she's developing a reputation that will follow her for years. Talk about his advice, including the statement, "You hang out with nice people, you get nice friends. . . . You hang out with yo-yo people, you get yo-yo friends" (1 Corinthians 15:33, Proverbs 12:26).

5. All of the main characters want to be respected. How does each attempt to gain that respect? Why is it that respect can't be *demanded;* it must be *earned?*

6. Proverbs 20:3 says, "It is to a man's honor to avoid strife." Though Rocky is a fighter, he tends to avoid strife and protect others. Recall as many scenes as you can in which he shows mercy, compassion, or forgiveness. Then ask, "Which instance impressed you most? Why?" Why does seeing Rocky extend grace to others make *his* shot at redemption that much easier to cheer?

7. Paulie is boorish, bitter, and childish. Why do you think Rocky remains friends with him? Adrian actually leaves home to escape her brother's abusiveness. Why is that smart? Why is she *unwise* to move in with Rocky? As her friend, what options might you have suggested?

8. How do Rocky's rigorous workouts compare to the spiritual training prescribed in 1 Corinthians 9:24-27? What steps are you taking to succeed in becoming more Christlike? Rocky had to deny himself certain things to build strength and stamina. In accordance with Mark 8:34 and Hebrews 12:1, are there things God has been telling you to lay aside?

9. Apply Proverbs 16:18 to the arrogant champ getting knocked down in the first round. Have you ever been humbled after getting a little cocky? What happened?

10. Rocky feels past his prime due to wasted years and missed opportunities. Regardless of your age, can you relate? If you haven't

already done so, resolve to start fresh. Draw encouragement from Philippians 3:13-14 and Joel 2:23-27. Then go for it!

Follow-Up Activity

No doubt your teen admired Rocky's ability to find beauty in the withdrawn, frumpy Adrian. In the weeks to come, look for opportunities to challenge your son or daughter to find beauty in ordinary things. Or better yet, things that have been broken or cast aside. For example, visit a used car lot, pick a vehicle at random and ask your teen to point out three cool things about it. The object is to get them past a potentially negative first impression, have them lay aside cynicism and a critical spirit, and focus on the positives. It might take them a while to answer your challenge. But the more they do this, the more it will come naturally—even when studying people.

Just for Fun

Because *Rocky* was shot on a tight budget (in just 28 days), the climactic bout was filmed backward beginning with round 15. That allowed the actors to start out in heavy makeup and have it removed gradually until they reached the opening bell.

—*Mick Silva*

Secondhand Lions

Rated: PG
Themes: Integrity, chivalry, perseverance, clinging to virtue, honesty, greed, appreciating the elderly, valuing people over money
Running Time: 1 hour, 50 minutes
Starring: Robert Duvall as Hub; Michael Caine as Garth; Haley Joel Osment as Walter; Kyra Sedgwick as Mae
Directed by: Tim McCanlies

Cautions

Some violence when Hub battles greasers and Mae's boyfriend assaults Walter. Action includes flurries of swashbuckling swordplay. Profanity is mild but common with about two dozen uses of "h—" or "d—n" and an indelicate reference to breast feeding.

Story Summary

This warm, humorous drama set in the early 1960s is about a boy who becomes a young man during a summer stranded with two crusty great-uncles in rural Texas.

Eager to begin a road trip alone, Walter's deceitful, avaricious mother, Mae, deposits him on her uncles' doorstep in hopes he can find the sacks of money rumored to be hidden on their land. The mousy 12-year-old isn't party to her greed. And he's no more interested in spending three months with these two strangers than they are in hosting him. There's no phone. No TV. All the aging McCann brothers do is sit on their rickety front porch, sip iced tea, and wait with shotguns in their laps for the

113

inevitable parade of gold-digging relatives and salesmen eager to separate them from their supposed fortune.

The McCanns grudgingly take Walter in. Garth is the more sensitive of the two, while Hub is a callous workhorse who, at one point, holds his own against four knife-wielding punks. Walter sleeps in their attic where he finds an old trunk pasted with travel labels from all over the world. Inside is the photo of a beautiful woman. Walter asks his Uncle Garth who she is. Garth spins a tale of how he and his adventure-seeking brother, Hub, journeyed to Europe, landed in the French Foreign Legion, rescued a maiden, and outsmarted a wealthy sheik. We see Garth's yarn played out in fun, episodic flashbacks crafted like old Saturday matinee serials. Chases. Sword fights. Swells of romantic music. The stories captivate the boy, creating a sense of wonder and adventure. But is Garth's incredible story true?

As for the ornery Hub, he's having a hard time coping with aging. He fears he's becoming a useless anachronism whose best days are behind him. A mild heart attack doesn't help matters.

The longer Walter spends with the McCanns, the more he appreciates them and has his imagination stimulated. Meanwhile, Walter inspires Hub and Garth to start enjoying their money. Their oddest indulgence is a used lioness from the circus. Decked out in safari gear, the brothers prepare to release the beast and hunt it down for sport, though she turns out to be a much better pet for Walter than "big game" for their fragile egos.

Summer wears on. The men soften and Walter comes out of his shell. Just when it seems they've bonded, gossipy locals cast aspersions on how the McCanns got so filthy rich. Did they rob a bank? Were they in league with the mob? Suddenly, a boy who has spent years enduring a mother's lies must wonder if his newfound heroes have feet of clay. The good news is that the McCanns are legit. The bad news is that Mae and her scurrilous boyfriend show up one night in search of the money. Walter's unwillingness to cooperate leads to conflict and a daring rescue by his pet lion. Walter ultimately decides that, although he loves his mom and hopes she can rebound from a pattern of poor choices, his best shot at a healthy life is with Hub and Garth. As for the money, Walter learns that the most valuable inheritance his great-uncles could leave him lies in their exotic stories and rich personalities.

One of 2002's best family films, *Secondhand Lions* reminds teens to value aging relatives as unique, substantive individuals with stories to tell and wisdom to impart. It also urges senior citizens to finish strong, build a bridge to the younger generation, and refuse to believe that their best years are behind them.

 ## Before You Watch

Casually ask teens, "What would you like to inherit from your grandparents?" Odds are they'll gravitate to physical possessions (a piece of jewelry, an heirloom, a special photo, a meaningful piece of furniture), which is normal in a culture that puts a lot of value on tangible items. File this away so that, after the film, you can revisit the subject by asking, "What *nonmaterial* things would you like to inherit from your grandparents?" That could include a skill, passion, character trait, etc.

Bible Bookmarks

Ps. 14:1-3; Isa. 64:6; Jn. 3:16; 1 Cor. 13; 1 Sam. 24, 26, and 16:7

Talking Points

1. Without a dad in his life, what was Walter missing that his uncles provided? Why is that important? Talk about Walter's relationship with his mom, and how her misplaced priorities contributed to his insecurities.

2. While Hub's contention that "men are basically good" reveals his noble desire to approach others without suspicion and cynicism, how does God view man's "goodness"? Read Psalm 14:1-3 and Isaiah 64:6. How is that different from our value in God's sight, expressed in John 3:16?

3. How are the McCann brothers—like the lioness—considered to be "defective" by those who see only the exterior and not the heart? Read 1 Samuel 16:7. Discuss ways we can be guilty of prejudging people that way today.

4. Contrast the swashbuckling action of Walter's imagination with the screen violence so prevalent in modern movies. What does that say about our culture?

5. Hub tells Walter there are some things in life we must believe in, whether or not they appear to be true or practical in the world around us: "Courage, honor, and virtue mean everything. Money and power mean nothing. Good always triumphs over evil, and true love never dies. Those are the things worth believing in." As Christians, what are some truths *we* must cling to, whether our culture values them or not?

6. Garth describes Hub's and Jasmine's attraction as "love at first sight." Is it possible to truly love someone after just one glance? Why or why not? Read the Bible's definition of love in 1 Corinthians 13.

7. How did you feel when Walter finally confronted his mother about her pattern of poor choices? Was he respectful? What can we learn from this scene about handling conflict?

8. Within Garth's tales, Hub is portrayed as a man of mercy. Compare the way Hub spares the life of the Arab ruler trying to kill him with the way David dealt with King Saul in 1 Samuel 24 and 26.

9. Too much alcohol (in the French bar) and Walter's introduction to chewing tobacco are shown to have consequences. What are they? Use this as an opportunity to talk about the temptation teens may feel to "experiment."

10. Of the two brothers, which do you respect more, Hub or Garth? Why?

11. Screenwriter Tim McCanlies finished writing *Secondhand Lions* a decade before it made it to the big screen. It might have taken less time, but he insisted on directing it himself, explaining, "I think a lot of people would have put Jim Carrey in this with old makeup and made it a stupid comedy. This is about something so important, and that is, 'What do we teach boys?'"[8] Explore that question together. What *does* our culture tell boys about who they should be and how they should behave? How does that differ from what Hub tells Walter? Discuss some biblical examples of true manliness, starting with Jesus Himself.

Follow-Up Activity

When our elders pass away, oftentimes so do their experiences and fascinating stories. Do you know aging relatives, friends, or neighbors who, like the McCanns, feel useless or just seem to be putting in time? What can you do to inspire them and make them feel valuable? It might be as simple as asking to hear their story. Teens willing to go the second mile can chronicle those experiences in a creative way, writing them down or putting together a scrapbook.

Just for Fun

Fans of the comic strips *Bloom County, Outland,* and *Opus* will find the style of adult Walter's artwork strangely familiar. That's because it was drawn specifically for the movie by the creator of those popular strips, Pulitzer Prize-winning cartoonist Berkeley Breathed.

—*Bob Smithouser*

Selena

Rated: PG
Themes: Pursuing dreams, handling prejudice, modest dress, perseverance, releasing children, the price of fame, forgiveness, betrayal, cooperation in marriage, living up to the expectations of others
Running Time: 2 hours, 8 minutes
Starring: Jennifer Lopez as Selena; Edward James Olmos as Abraham; Constance Marie as Marcela; Jon Seda as Chris
Directed by: Gregory Nava

Cautions

The primary hurdle for families will be the provocative costumes Selena wears on stage, and possibly some mildly sensual Latin dancing. Parents of boys in particular may want to scan those scenes in advance to determine appropriateness. There is also brief alcohol use and a few profanities.

Story Summary

At age nine, Selena Quintanilla didn't know she had a gift.
Nor did she know that her discovery of it would result in a successful music career, marriage to a member of her band, numerous awards . . . and an untimely death. This is the bittersweet true story of that beloved Tejano singer, whose tragic end VH1 compared to the losses of Elvis Presley and John Lennon.

After meeting Selena briefly before one of her last concerts, we are swept back to 1961 to watch her father's Mexican-American doo-wop trio struggle to find an audience. Prejudice cuts both ways in Abraham's

119

home state of Texas. He and his friends face racial discrimination from whites, while ethnic crowds won't accept them because their tunes aren't Mexican enough ("That's gringo music! . . . We want to dance!"). We catch up with Abe 20 years later. He has set aside artistic ambitions and settled into a stable job that offers his wife, Marcela, the suburban security she wants for their three children.

One day Abe is blown away by his nine-year-old daughter's singing voice. Selena revives dormant dreams in her father, who impulsively buys used instruments and forces his complaining brood to practice '50s tunes in the living room. Then he opens a Mexican restaurant to showcase them, and teaches Selena to sing in Spanish to connect her with that side of her heritage. But when Abe loses his day job and the business goes bust, they must sell the house and move in with relatives.

With nothing more to lose, the Quintanillas pursue music full-time. The kids endure a rocky start on the county fair circuit, but they stick with it and improve. By the late '80s they are traveling by bus and performing original songs as Selena and Los Dinos. As the crowds grow, the 18-year-old lead singer's wardrobe shrinks. Dad is furious. He chastises Selena about indecency before compromising. Clearly, Abe is having a hard time watching his little girl grow up.

More concerts. A chart-topping single. Public appearances. Selena even visits Mexico and wins over that skeptical culture with her charm. Now in full manager mode, Abe controls his daughter's every move. But he can't control her heart. Tension builds when Selena falls for Chris, the band's streetwise new guitarist. It's clear that he loves her too, but Abe can't respect the young man's heavy-metal roots (especially after Chris's buddies trash a hotel room). Subtle flirtations get under Abe's skin. He blows up and fires Chris, forcing the couple to meet on the sly. Then they elope. That rebellious act actually has a calming effect, and the Quintanillas welcome Chris into the family . . . and back into the band.

Selena is now happy and in her element as an artist. As popular as ever, she plans an English-language crossover CD, and even fulfills her dream of opening a salon and designing fashions. Indeed, when this queen of Tejano music walks off with a Grammy for Best Mexican-American Album, it seems all of her dreams will come true.

Then, tragedy. Abe learns that money is missing from the boutique. The trail leads to Selena's business manager and fan club president, Yolanda Saldivar. They confront her about the shortfall and some missing documents. Soon after, TV stations break the news that the 23-year-old international superstar has been slain by her desperate, disturbed associate. The film ends on a sad note with images of fans at a candlelight memorial and vibrant archival footage of the real Selena.

 ## Before You Watch

Released posthumously, Selena's 1995 CD *Dreaming of You* went to No. 1 and has sold more than 3 million copies. If your family doesn't own that album or the movie soundtrack, try to find a copy and listen to it prior to your Movie Night. Even a passing familiarity with the songs will make this film biography (which uses the singer's original recordings) even more meaningful.

Bible Bookmarks

Eph. 5:22-33; 1 Pet. 3:3-4; Matt. 5:28, 15:4; 2 Sam. 11:2-5; Ps. 139:23-24; Phil. 2:3

Talking Points

1. Abe and Marcela have different dreams and personalities that clash at times, but can also complement each other. Cite three cases in which this divergence created conflict, and three in which that balance moved the family in a positive direction. How well does each spouse fulfill his or her part of Ephesians 5:22-33?

2. Selena's dad persuades her mom that a band will give the family something special to do together. What hobbies, games, or other activities are special in your home? Is there something you'd love to do together, but never mentioned because you feared a reaction like the

one Abe got? Agree to try new things for each other.

3.   Abraham comes unglued upon seeing Selena dancing in skimpy outfits ("She's practically got nothing on! She's in her bra! . . . There are *men* out here!). Mom defends her with the same arguments a teen girl might use. Who is right according to 1 Peter 3:3-4? Is it easy for a woman to dress modestly in our culture? Why or why not? Why is it to everyone's advantage that she does (Matthew 5:28, 2 Samuel 11:2-5)?

4.   Abe's own dashed dreams find an outlet in Selena. In what other ways do parents try to live through their children? Is this healthy? Why or why not? How can it lead to the kind of rebellion Chris describes ("If I'da been in your family then I'da been a doctor.")?

5.   Although Chris wasn't actively involved in the hotel room fiasco, he was still to blame. Why? In what other ways do we commit "sins of omission"?

6.   Talk about the romance shared by Selena and Chris. What did you admire about their interaction? How did you feel when Abe tried to end their relationship? Put yourself in Abe's place, then in Selena's. Does Matthew 15:4 apply to this situation?

7.   Abe complains about the exhausting expectations placed on Mexican-Americans to be "twice as perfect as anybody else." Do you ever feel, because of certain attitudes in the church and others in the world, that Christians are expected to be twice as perfect as everyone else? How so? Why is it even harder for pastors' kids?

8.   Abe tells Selena, "You gotta be who you are." Who are *you?* How has God wired you (personality, likes/dislikes, talents, dreams, etc.), and how is that different from the labels that can define you (student, son/daughter, employee)? Why is it important to know the difference? Let Psalm 139:23-24 be your prayer as you attempt to balance exploring your uniqueness while striving to be Christlike.

9.   Read Philippians 2:3 and name some of the ways Selena maintained perspective and treated others with respect. Can you think of a current celebrity who seems to have the same attitude? Are there others who don't? Does this impact how you feel about an entertainer?

 ## Follow-Up Activity

Take your teen to dinner and ask, "What was symbolic about Selena's daring bungee jump?" Let them wrestle with it. Then clarify that, after years of having her life managed for her, she was frustrated and desperate to exert some control—even if that meant doing something impulsive and potentially dangerous. Get a feel for how desperate your teen may be to exert similar control. Do they feel stifled by the fact that someone (maybe you, maybe even God) has been pulling most of the strings in their life?

Even compliant Christian young people can reach that point. In some, the need to feel more in charge manifests itself in uncharacteristic acts of irresponsibility. Others become full-blown prodigals. By making them aware of this in a relaxed way, you may be able to head off trouble or simply remind them of your faith in their ability to make good choices. Are you more controlling than you think? Let your teen be very honest (respectful, but honest). Don't be defensive. Then come up with ways to loosen your grip and allow for a happier, more empowered soon-to-be adult.

Just for Fun

Jon Seda was an amateur boxer before turning to acting. He posted a record of 21-1 and was runner-up in the New Jersey Golden Gloves competition.

—Mick Silva

Signs

Rated: PG-13
Themes: Crisis of faith, cherishing family, forgiveness, confronting evil, the notion that all things happen for a reason, recovering from loss
Running Time: 1 hour, 46 minutes
Starring: Mel Gibson as Rev. Graham Hess; Joaquin Phoenix as Merrill Hess; Rory Culkin as Morgan; Abigail Breslin as Bo
Directed by: M. Night Shyamalan

Cautions

Of the dozen-or-so profanities or crude expressions, the worst is an exclamation of "bulls—" from Morgan (hit mute right after his father says, "My vote counts as two"). In addition to two violent confrontations with an alien (no humans are injured), sudden jolts ratchet up the tension. The sheriff describes an accident victim's fatal injuries.

Story Summary

Six months ago Father Graham Hess lost his wife. While walking along a country road not far from their Pennsylvania farm, she was struck and pinned to a tree when a neighbor fell asleep at the wheel. Graham arrived just in time to say good-bye. As her life ebbed away, so did his faith in God. Bitter, Graham left the ministry. With the help of his brother Merrill (a washed-up minor league slugger), he's now trying to raise his asthmatic son, Morgan, and angelic little girl, Bo, a child strangely paranoid about the condition of her drinking water.

One morning the children discover a disturbance in their cornfield. Countless healthy stalks have been bent over, creating large symbols in the field. Graham assumes it's a hoax. Then a dark figure appears on their roof. Pranksters? A disturbed drifter? The search for rational explanations is interrupted by news of patterns like the ones in their field showing up worldwide. Morgan is fascinated by the possibility that aliens may be communicating with each other via these crop circles, as well as by radio signals he has picked up on Bo's baby monitor. Riveting new television reports show lights hovering above Mexico City. If they *are* extraterrestrials, are they ambassadors of peace or hostile invaders?

Graham can't muster much passion for the curious events. The still-grieving widower, having cut loose his spiritual anchors, is emotionally numb and spiritually adrift. If God exists, does He care about lights in the sky? Or ministers' wives? It's a bitter pill.

After engaging his miracle-believing brother on the issue of providence versus luck, Graham concludes defiantly, "There is no one watching out for us, Merrill. We are all on our own."

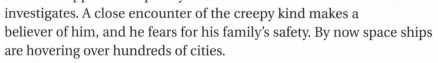

Over the next few days, Morgan and Bo study up on UFOs. Merrill stays glued to the TV set. A cryptic phone call sends Graham to the home of Ray Reddy, the man whose carelessness led to his wife's death. Still wracked with guilt, Ray apologizes to Graham and casually mentions that there's an alien trapped in his pantry. Graham investigates. A close encounter of the creepy kind makes a believer of him, and he fears for his family's safety. By now space ships are hovering over hundreds of cities.

The Hesses seek shelter in their home, boarding up the doors and windows. A dinner of comfort foods leads to a meltdown when Morgan suggests they pray. "I am not wasting one more minute of my life on prayer," Graham growls. Amid shouting and tears, he breaks down and everyone embraces. The group hug is short-lived. The invasion has begun. With creatures closing in, they all retreat into the basement. A crippling asthma attack eventually forces the family out of their hiding place to retrieve Morgan's medicine. The unearthly confrontation that follows leaves Graham convinced that God has not forsaken him, and that everything happens for a reason.

Beyond its nail-nibbling sci-fi plot, *Signs* is about a family pulling together and a man grappling with philosophical and spiritual questions that cut to our very core. All ends well . . . sort of. Due to the story's ambiguous theology, it's uncertain what Graham's restored faith is really in. Does he have a bond with God that could now survive Job-like tragedy? Or will he pull the collar off again if things turn sour? If only we could be sure that Father Hess's windblown faith is in God's remarkable, unchanging character rather than mere circumstances and signs.

Before You Watch

The day of your Movie Night, read Psalm 46 during family devotions, or independently as part of your personal quiet time. Meditate on what it says about God's character and His reliability as our "fortress" in times of trouble.

Chat with your teen about aliens and UFOs. Do you think life exists on other planets? What kind? If it did, why wouldn't that change anything about God's relationship with us as set forth in Scripture?

Bible Bookmarks

Mk. 8:11-13; Job 1:18-22, 2:9-10; 1 Thess. 5:17-18; Rom. 8:28; Jer. 17:7-8; Isa. 40:28-31; Jn. 14:27, 15:4; Lk. 14:25-35; Prov. 15:29; Matt. 6:6; 2 Cor. 1:3-4; 1 Pet. 1:3-9; Jas. 1:2-4; Ps. 34:18

Talking Points

1. Did a scene give you the creeps or make you jump? Discuss what you like or dislike about scary movies in general, and how they've changed over time. Would you agree that what we don't see can be more frightening than what we do see? Why? How does that apply to *Signs*?

2. What behavior indicated that the members of the Hess family truly loved each other, especially siblings Morgan and Bo?

3.   Do you agree with the film's premise that everything happens for a reason? On what basis? How is believing in "no coincidences" different from the promise of Romans 8:28?

4.   Did it bother you to hear Graham lashing out at God? Since the Lord knows our hearts anyway, do you think it's okay to vent our emotions? Why or why not? Contrast Graham's reaction to losing a family member with Job's reaction (Job 1:18-22) and how, in the wake of tragedy and pain, Job refused to curse God (2:9-10).

5.   Merrill chides Graham, "One thing I can't take is when my older brother, who's everything I want to be, starts losing faith in things." Who is watching you as you live for Jesus? Do you find it hard to be authentic and honest, and at the same time measure up to someone's expectations? *Note: This dynamic can create enormous stress in a young person's life.*

6.   Tossed about by circumstances and emotions, Graham fails to lean on the bedrock of Scripture and an understanding of God's character. Read Jeremiah 17:7-8, Isaiah 40:28-31, and John 15:4. How might deeper intimacy with the Lord have prepared him to face hard times?

7.   If an "idol" is anything more precious to us than the Lord, what had become an idol to Graham? *(Hint: In crisis, prayer is replaced with soothing memories of his children's births; spiritual stability is contingent on the health of family members.)* How can idolizing something good (family, work, a hobby, etc.) create an unhealthy imbalance in our lives? Read Luke 14:25-35. What thing, if taken away, might cause you to react as Graham did? Why? What does that tell you?

8.   Compare Graham's bitterness toward God with Morgan's anger toward Graham at the dinner table. How are the venomous accusations similar ("I hate you. . . . You let Mom die.")? Later, when Morgan can't breathe, how does Graham's intervention mirror God's desire to comfort His children? Have you ever felt the Lord telling you to lay aside fear and "believe" amid stress or anxiety? What happened?

9.   The film emphasizes the significance of *signs* and *outcomes*. God cares more about *faith* and *process*. Why do you think Jesus downplays the value of signs in Mark 8:11-13? Explore God's desire to walk through trials with us in order to calm us (John 14:27), comfort us (2 Corinthians 1:3-4), refine us, and instill joy (James 1:2-4, 1 Peter 1:3-9).

10. At one point, Graham stubbornly refuses to pray. Have you ever struggled to talk to God? Why? How would you respond to a friend who

told you that prayer is a waste of time? (See Matthew 6:6, Proverbs 15:29, 1 Thessalonians 5:17-18, Psalm 34:18.)

11. Take a minute to compile two lists: movies presenting aliens as friendly, and those portraying them as warring invaders. Why do filmmakers take such diverse approaches? Classic alien invasion flicks such as *The Day the Earth Stood Still* and *Invasion of the Body Snatchers* had obvious social/political subtexts. Does *Signs?* Do other sci-fi films you've seen?

Follow-Up Activity

If your teen is curious about space exploration and what we know about the galaxy, spend time together reading about its history (solarviews.com/eng/history.htm) as well as recent developments (click on "what's new"). Be sure to check out the cool photos!

Just for Fun

Culkin says he enjoyed teasing Breslin—the little sister he never had—on the set. Breslin said, "He makes me say, 'King Rory, you are my lord and master.'"[9] She should be used to such playful harassment since she probably gets some from her real-life big brother, actor Spencer Breslin.

—Bob Smithouser

Sky Captain and the World of Tomorrow

Rated: PG
Themes: Loyalty, honesty, forgiveness, self-sacrifice, romantic love, ordering priorities
Running Time: 1 hour, 46 minutes
Starring: Jude Law as Joe "Sky Captain" Sullivan; Gwyneth Paltrow as Polly Perkins; Giovanni Ribisi as Dex Dearborn; Angelina Jolie as Franky
Directed by: Kerry Conran

Cautions

Flurries of sci-fi action and combat violence. The few casualties include a scientist being reduced to a skeleton by an electric force field, and Joe and Polly finishing off a pesky android. We see a decayed corpse. Ten uses of either "h—," "d—n," or "oh my god." After being knocked out cold, three characters awaken in bed to find themselves relieved of their clothes (nothing explicit or sexual).

Story Summary

If you're in the mood for a breezy, action-packed, retro sci-fi adventure (think "Movie Night lite"), *Sky Captain* is a fun, visually distinctive popcorn flick inspired by old comic books, B-movie serials, and '40s film noir.

It's 1939. Renowned scientists who worked at a secret facility outside of Berlin prior to WWI are disappearing without a trace. The last of them, Dr. Jennings, sends a cryptic note to reporter Polly Perkins asking to meet in a darkened theater where he warns her of a man named Totenkopf. Air raid sirens blare. Suddenly an army of giant flying robots descends on New York City and marches through the streets in search of generators powering the metropolis. Polly dodges the iron behemoths and nearly gets squashed, save for the heroics of flyboy Joe "Sky Captain" Sullivan, who swoops down in his tricked-out fighter plane. It appears that Joe and Polly share a stormy history.

In search of answers, Polly visits the air base headquarters of Joe and his gadget-inventing sidekick, Dex. The reunion is tense, the pair's mutual distrust palpable. Still, Polly and Joe realize they need each other in order to figure out who is behind the global rash of robot invasions. They arrive at Dr. Jennings's ransacked lab just in time for Joe to battle an intruder and for a dying Dr. Jennings to entrust Polly with two vials that mustn't fall into the wrong hands.

A squadron of futuristic fighters attacks the air base. Joe and Polly jump into his cockpit and engage in an aerial dogfight that quickly turns into a cat-and-mouse chase among New York City high-rises. While they're busy in the air, Dex pinpoints a crucial radio signal and leaves Joe a clue about its origin before being abducted by metal marauders with serpentine limbs. Dex's clue leads Joe and Polly to an abandoned mining outpost in Tibet where they narrowly escape an explosive situation, but not before bad guys seize the vials.

Returning to the sky, the photo-snapping journalist and her two-timing ex-boyfriend bicker with a passion that betrays the feelings they still have for one another. Polly soon meets the "other woman" when they lay over at an airborne reconnaissance outpost run by British officer Captain Francesca "Franky" Cook. Before we know it, planes are morphing into an amphibious force and challenging mechanized sentries guarding an undersea tunnel that empties into a jungle inhabited by bizarre creatures.

Joe and Polly maneuver through the dense vegetation until they dis-cover a high-tech fortress where all of earth's animals are being loaded onto a rocket in pairs. It seems the elusive Totenkopf has a God complex.

He plans to launch an "ark" into space, destroy all life on Earth, and start over. After reconnecting with Dex and several missing scientists, the troupe learns that Totenkopf is actually dead, and that his automated system is carrying out its programming. Joe sets off alone on what he realizes is a suicide mission. Lucky for him, Polly tags along. The couple defeat the mysterious woman (an android in disguise), save the world, and rekindle their romantic flame.

Aside from 26 days spent shooting actors in front of a blue screen, *Sky Captain* was created entirely inside a computer. No locations. No sets. No extras. The result is a film with a bold visual style emphasizing sparse sepia tones and strategic injections of color. Star Jude Law was eager to be part of the project for the same reason families will cheer it: "I just thought it was about time someone took us back to a science-fiction genre that's without cynicism, that's more innocent and optimistic."[10]

Before You Watch

One source of inspiration for *Sky Captain* was Orson Welles's famous "War of the Worlds" radio broadcast of Oct. 30, 1938. (Part of Polly's phoned-in account of the encroaching robots comes directly from that script.) Track down a copy, perhaps through your local library. Listen together as a family. Talk about how that sci-fi chiller about a Martian invasion—played straight—created alarm (for more visit www.war-ofthe-worlds.co.uk/radio.htm or pick up *The Panic Broadcast,* a book about the event authored by the man who wrote the radio script, Howard Koch).

Teens take for granted the wealth of cable news channels, Web sites, and other outlets offering split-second information. With limited media options, people of that era had a hard time confirming that Welles's 1938 Halloween eve program wasn't a real newscast. How would the public respond to a similar hoax today? Does that mean we can't be manipulated? What types of media tricks are distinctly modern? Talk about shrewdly edited "reality" shows, digitally altered photos, etc.—and how to guard against being duped.

Bible Bookmarks

Ps. 33:18-22, 101:3; Phil. 4:8; Col. 2:8; Gen. 6-9; Rom. 15:12-13; Prov. 3:5-6; Jn. 15:13

Talking Points

1. Some passages of Scripture are models to be imitated. Others are simply accounts of how God chose to operate in a specific situation. Genesis 6-9 is the latter, though Totenkopf decided that "cleansing" the earth and starting fresh was an idea whose time had come . . . again. Together, come up with four things Jesus did that we should do also. Then think of four things He did that He never intended us to imitate.

2. Trying to justify his actions, Totenkopf said, "I have been witness to a world bent on hatred and doomed to self-destruction." We could say the same of our world today. Ask, "What would be a healthy plan for turning things around? On a smaller scale, what can you do to make *your* world (at school, home, church, in the neighborhood, etc.) a better place?" Offer to help make it happen.

3. Polly and Joe share an attraction but they don't trust each other. How does that reduce the odds of them having a successful relationship? Likewise, we may be drawn to God but unless we put our trust in Him, our spiritual romance won't be solid. Read Psalm 33:18-22, Romans 15:12-13, and Proverbs 3:5-6.

4. Share John 15:13 and cite instances in the film where people risked life and limb for each other, or for the mission as a whole.

5. The mutated man in Tibet asks Joe to put him out of his misery. Talk about the issue of mercy killing or euthanasia, and why *all* life is sacred to God.

6. Were there moments when you thought a "good guy" might betray Joe and Polly? Who? Why were you suspicious? *Sky Captain* harkens back to a less cynical age when characters could be taken at face value. Discuss how postmodern entertainment has conditioned us to be on the lookout for double-crossers and hidden agendas. Is this healthy? Why or why not?

7. Polly's editor worries that she'll be walking into danger at the theater. She replies, "It's only a movie," which sounds a lot like the response teens give cautious parents before heading off to the multiplex. Talk about the need to watch movies with discernment. Apply Psalm 101:3, Philippians 4:8, and Colossians 2:8.

 ## Follow-Up Activity

With one exposure left, Polly turns down worthy options to secure the photo *most* important to her. Help your teen

134

bring priorities into focus with a fun exercise. Ask them to list 16 things they love, in no particular order. Sports. Foods. Hobbies. Family traditions. Bands. Movies. School activities. God. There are no right or wrong answers. Then *you* transfer those 16 responses into a bracket like those used for single-elimination sports tournaments (shown below). Different "passions" will face off head-to-head, tournament style. Have your teen choose a winner in each match-up and explain why. For example, "pizza" may defeat "skiing" in the first round and advance to challenge the winner of "weekends at the beach" vs. "trimming the Christmas tree." As your teenager gets closer to a champion, their priorities will unfold before their eyes. *(Note: It will work best if "God" and "Family" appear on opposite sides of the bracket and if "Family" is treated as a whole, not divided into individual family members.)*

This is the right half of a sample "priority bracket." Another eight passions would square off on the left side, leading to the winner from each side meeting in the championship round.

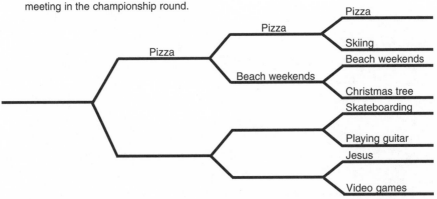

Just for Fun

Sky Captain contains embedded nods to classic movies, including *Godzilla, The Empire Strikes Back, King Kong, The War of the Worlds,* and George Lucas's *THX 1138.* See how many you can find!

—*Bob Smithouser*

135

Spellbound

Rated: G
Themes: Hard work, perseverance, sportsmanship, support of family, discipline, daring to be different, handling defeat, overcoming circumstances
Running Time: 1 hour, 37 minutes
Starring: Real-life spellers Harry Altman, Angela Arenivar, Ted Brigham, April DeGideo, Neil Kadakia, Nupur Lala, Emily Stagg, and Ashley White
Directed by: Jeffrey Blitz

Cautions

There are a few exclamations of "oh my god." After misspelling a word, an anonymous competitor says "crap."

Story Summary

America's fascination with "reality TV" spawned a growing number of prime-time shows pandering to the worst in human nature. Greed. Deception. Cutthroat competition. Unscrupulous romantic pursuits. Manufactured domestic strife. For families that enjoy raw, unscripted drama, but are sick and tired of scandalous TV shows exploiting immorality and social cruelty, this delightful film will be a breath of fresh air.

Not to be confused with the Alfred Hitchcock thriller of the same title about an amnesiac who holds the key to an unsolved murder, this *Spellbound* is an Oscar-nominated documentary about teenagers with *exceptional* memories who hold the key to questions like "How do you spell 'peptidoglycan'?" It follows eight bright, driven, decent young

137

people from diverse backgrounds as they compete for the grand prize in the 1999 Scripps Howard National Spelling Bee.

If the notion of watching an adolescent sweat over the correct spelling of "banns" sounds about as exciting as watching an ice cube melt, don't write it off too quickly. You'll miss out on a small treasure. The *Chicago Tribune* wrote, "*Spellbound* boasts all of the drama and suspense of any reality TV show, but it actually stars smart people. And they're kids." *Rolling Stone* remarked, "By the time they're onstage, your pulse is pounding right along with theirs. Spell this movie: g-r-e-a-t." Indeed, *Spellbound* is a lot more engaging than a movie about dictionary memorization and etymology has any right to be, primarily because everyone onscreen is so easy to root for.

The studious teens at the center of the action include a wealthy East Indian boy whose father hires the best tutors he can find, a Bible-believing African-American girl from the projects, a hyperactive nerd with no inner monologue, and the daughter of non-English-speaking Mexican immigrants who were so desperate to give their children a U.S. education that they once tried to cross the border illegally. Those teens and other key competitors hail from all over the country. They have nerves of steel and share a work ethic that's second to none.

Every year nine million students participate in spelling bees. The 249 regional champs advance to the World Series of spelling in Washington, D.C. Only one wins. And all it takes to be eliminated is a single misspoken letter. Talk about pressure. You'll feel bad that *any* of these likable kids has to lose. Still, it's encouraging to see how they handle defeat. One girl says after bowing out, "I already feel like a champion just getting here. I think that's enough because a lot of people don't even accomplish that." That attitude is fairly typical. Indeed, because the filmmakers seem to agree that they're *all* winners, we get a sympathetic, victorious take on each child's experience rather than an invasive look at tantrums, heartbreak, or parental bitterness.

Although *Spellbound* was edged out for Best Documentary at the 2003 Oscars, it won six other top industry awards for documentary filmmaking. Whether your teenager is driven to excel at academics, athletics, or the arts, this wholesome, unscripted nail-biter contains plenty of lessons for students and adults alike.

 ## Before You Watch

During the week prior to your Movie Night, watch several "reality" programs on TV. Avoid any with explicit content, but don't resist those that are merely sensational, cynical, mean-spirited, or morally ambiguous. While such shows might not ordinarily meet your family standard, viewing them as a precursor to *Spellbound* will help teens distinguish between filmmakers out to exploit their subjects and shock their audience, and those who want to celebrate the best in people in order to inspire viewers.

Bible Bookmarks

Gal. 5:16-26; Phil. 4:6-7; 1 Pet. 5:6-7; Jn. 14:6

Talking Points

1. If you performed the "Before You Watch" activity, invite teens to compare and contrast the reality shows you watched against this documentary. How are the goals and attitudes of the producers different? What did each want you to feel about people and circumstances they portrayed? Apply specific components of Galatians 5:16-26 to what you observed.

2. In the DVD commentary, the filmmakers discuss the challenge of shooting hours of footage, then cobbling together a few minutes' worth to tell a compelling story that's also truthful and fair. Read the following comments aloud and share your reaction to them: "Particularly in the [editing] process it gets really problematic because you're making choices all the time. . . . You can make anybody a devil or a saint. We tried very hard to be honest with these stories, but also it's part of just

139

how charming each of these kids was that we kind of fell in love with them and felt protective and didn't want to distort their stories. . . . There were probably ways of making our audience laugh not with them but at them. We had a rule about that, actually, which was 'Either the kid is making the joke or they would find it funny.'"

3. Which spellers did you find yourselves rooting for? Why? Were there any who *didn't* have your support? What made you disinclined to root for certain teens?

4. Ask your teen which *parents* they admired most and why. Although the moms and dads had different ways of showing it, all stood by their kids. Parents: How well are *you* doing in this area? If you're prepared for an honest answer, ask, "On a scale of 1 to 10, how well do you feel I'm supporting you? Why?" Then, "What would it take to reach a 10?"

5. Which do you think would be more stressful, competing in the bee yourself or watching helplessly while a loved one competed? Give specific reasons. Point to Philippians 4:6-7 and 1 Peter 5:6-7 as sources of strength and comfort when the heat is on.

6. Neil is a practicing Hindu. Ashley refers to herself as a "prayer warrior." And although Georgie Thampy isn't one of the film's primary subjects, he is an outspoken born-again Christian. Read John 14:6 and discuss the different faiths that appear in the movie.

7. What did you think of Ted's statement, "I don't think I'll win, but I'll try hard anyways. It will be fun either way, though"? (See whether your teen gravitates to the boy's pessimism, work ethic, or desire to enjoy the process.)

8. Reflecting on his elimination, Harry blames the official for mispronouncing his word. How did it make you feel to hear him say that?

9. After coming up short, Neil mentions having set a series of goals, and focuses on the ones he *did* reach. Why is this healthier than taking an all-or-nothing approach to competition? How can you apply this philosophy to your life?

Follow-Up Activity

Find out how good a speller you are with a little friendly competition. Grab a dictionary and take turns trying to stump each other. The only rule is that the person choosing the word has to pick it from the page he or she opens the book to. Whichever of you spells a given number of words correctly wins.

For nearly every speller featured in the movie, a dedicated teacher was cheering them on and offering guidance. Take a day or two to think about good teachers who impacted your lives. Each of you choose five and rank them in order. Get together and discuss why you ranked them as you did. (If your child has been home-schooled, feel free to broaden the field to include Sunday-school teachers or other adults in their lives.) As critical as a parent's love and encouragement are, why do you think it's important to know that someone *outside* the family believes in you? Look at your top picks. Have you ever told those teachers how much they impacted you? Maybe it's not too late to return the gift of encouragement.

Just for Fun

Behind the scenes, the producers asked each teen to share his or her all-time favorite word. The typical response was some bizarre, multisyllabic term no one had ever heard of before. But not Ashley, the Christian girl from Washington, D.C. Her answer was "love," inspiring one of the filmmakers to say, "That just showed us this weird sort of wisdom she had, even at that age."

—Bob Smithouser

Spider-Man

Rated: PG-13
Themes: Heroism, good vs. evil, social responsibility, loyalty, bullying, unrequited love, making hard choices, coping with loss
Running Time: 2 hours
Starring: Tobey Maguire as Peter Parker; Kirsten Dunst as Mary Jane Watson; Willem Dafoe as Norman Osborn; James Franco as Harry Osborn; Rosemary Harris as Aunt Mae
Directed by: Sam Raimi

 ## Cautions

Spider-Man is a coming-of-age superhero saga best viewed by mature teens. Violence ranges from hand-to-hand combat and abusive pro wrestling moves to several fatalities (characters get hurled through glass, blown up, impaled, and reduced to skeletons). A few shots of immodestly dressed women may be a spoiler for some families. Wrestling "babes" show a lot of skin. Mary Jane wears a few low-cut tops that reveal cleavage. As Spidey rescues her from back-alley thugs in the rain, viewers may want to skip ahead to avoid images of Dunst (sans bra) in a wet blouse. Profanity is mostly "a—," "h—," and exclamations of "oh my god," though there are two unfortunate uses of Jesus' name.

 ## Story Summary

Bespectacled nice guy Peter Parker can't catch a break. The nerdy teen is jeered by classmates and harassed by bullies. Even wealthy pal Harry hits on his secret crush, Mary Jane, and resents Peter a little for unintentionally usurping his father's respect ("I think he

143

wants to adopt you," Harry quips). Then, during a field trip, a genetically altered spider bites Peter on the hand. All adolescents face physical changes, but nothing like what Peter is about to experience.

After passing out at the home of guardians Uncle Ben and Aunt Mae, Peter awakens with an enhanced body. Lightning-fast reflexes. Wall-crawling agility. Increased strength. The ability to spin webs from his wrists and swing from them like an urban Tarzan. It's all overwhelming at first, but he corrals those talents and tries to parlay them into cash by entering a seedy wrestling match as the Human Spider. After being denied prize money by the promoter, he spitefully lets a robber get away with the gate receipts.

Then tragedy strikes. He meets up with Uncle Ben, only to discover that his father figure has been fatally shot by a carjacker—the very thief Peter let escape moments before.

Elsewhere in the thriving metropolis, Harry's corporate tycoon/scientist father, Norman Osborn, is desperate to secure a government contract for Oscorp. But his attempts to develop a performance-enhancing drug have met with limited success. Forced to produce results immediately, Norman tests the formula on himself. The experiment goes awry, generating a monstrous, Jekyll-Hyde fury that results in the death of a colleague . . . and the birth of a deranged villain known as the Green Goblin.

Plagued with guilt over his uncle's death, Peter elects to use his superpowers to fight crime and serve the greater good. Soon the name Spider-Man is on everyone's lips and on the front pages of newspapers throughout New York City. Some call him a hero. Others, including the *Daily Bugle*'s cranky, cynical editor, cast him as a vigilante menace. But when the Green Goblin starts wreaking havoc, it's clear only one person can stop him.

The Goblin's first move is to eliminate Oscorp's competition for the military contract—literally. Business improves, but Norman's status doesn't. His board decides to sell Oscorp and oust him. Looking like a deranged Power Ranger, Norman's masked alter ego goes on a vengeful rampage during a public festival. He incinerates unfaithful board members before being driven off by Spider-Man, who makes a strong impression on Mary Jane by saving her life.

Peter and Harry's friendship is complicated when Harry and Mary Jane become an item. Things get far worse when Norman uncovers his masked foe's secret identity and, amid ebbing sanity, strikes out at those close to Peter. The Goblin terrorizes Aunt Mae, then forces Spidey to choose between saving Mary Jane and rescuing a cable car full of children. The adversaries' final showdown ends with the Goblin accidentally killing himself while trying to impale Spider-Man.

One of the reasons the film works so well is that only half of the conflict takes place in comic book-style action sequences. The rest occurs within the multidimensional characters. In the end, Peter must live with the knowledge that his best friend blames Spider-Man for his father's death and has sworn revenge. And when the girl of his dreams confesses her love, he feels compelled (with the selfless conviction of 2 Timothy 2:4) to pass up romance in order to fulfill his noble calling. Because with great power comes great responsibility.

Before You Watch

Have you ever had an unrequited romantic crush or been attracted to the same person as your best friend? Most of us have. What happened? Talk about the butterflies or awkwardness. Young people experiencing such romantic challenges can feel alone and insecure—especially if they've endured rejection in the past. Before watching Peter Parker go through it, see if your teen has any feelings about the issue.

Bible Bookmarks

Lk. 9:1-6, 10:17-20; 1 Cor. 7:7, 12:4-11; Ps. 14:2; Matt. 25:40; Jas. 1:2-4; 2 Cor. 1:3-11, 11:13-15; Heb. 11:38; 2 Tim. 2:4; 1 Pet. 4:10; Phil. 4:13

Talking Points

1. How do you think Peter felt early in the film as a social outcast? How did his self-image change once he realized he had special powers? It's emboldening to know that we are armed with Jesus' divine authority (Luke 9:1-6, 10:17-20; Philippians 4:13). Also, consider which spiritual "superpowers" may be lurking within your teen (1 Corinthians 7:7, 12:4-11) and how to wield them (1 Peter 4:10).

2. Peter concludes that a gift can also be a curse. Do you agree? Offer some real-life examples. How can you limit the downside?

3. Compare the home environments of Peter, Mary Jane, and Harry. How does each relate differently to their parent or guardian? What difference does it make if an adult is absent/overbearing (Norman), belittling/argumentative (M. J.'s dad) or loving/patient (Ben and Mae)?

4. Ben says, "These are the years when a man changes into the man he's going to become the rest of his life." Do you agree? Read Psalm 14:2. What does God see in *you*? How might your actions better line up with your beliefs?

5. Peter selfishly lets the robber go, stating, "I missed the part where that's my problem." But it soon *becomes* his problem. In what other ways do people turn their backs and not do the right thing in life, thinking it won't impact them? Why, according to Matthew 25:40, is that an irresponsible attitude, especially for a Christian?

6. Losing Ben is a turning point for Peter. How can God use trials and tragedies to teach us about life, as well as His ability to comfort, heal, and strengthen us (James 1:2-4; 2 Corinthians 1:3-11)? Have you faced a life-changing trial? How did you feel? How has God used it in your life?

7. Some people think comic book stories about vigilante superheroes are wrong because they glamorize individuals taking justice into their own hands. Others see value in them. What's your opinion?

8. Much like the Green Goblin, our nemesis, Satan, also disguises his identity and tries to lure us to his side (2 Corinthians 11:13-15). Discuss ways he does that.

9. Spidey is misunderstood by some and persecuted by others. The Goblin tempts our discouraged hero to quit, saying, "In spite of everything you've done for them, they will hate you." Might Satan have used a similar line against Jesus heading to the cross? Consider our need to—

appreciated or not—serve Christ and others just like the martyrs honored in Hebrews 11 (11:38 says, "the world was not worthy of them").

10. Before initiating a heart-to-heart with Peter, Ben says, "Something's bothering him. Maybe he's too embarrassed to tell me what it is. Maybe I'm too embarrassed to ask him." As a parent, have you felt that way recently? Use this as an opportunity to invite your teen to open up about an issue he or she has been reluctant to discuss.

Follow-Up Activity

If you want to know how the saga continues, rent *Spider-Man 2* for your next Movie Night. Try developing your *own* curriculum that builds on this experience. Aside from a brutally violent operating room scene (surgeons trying to sever mechanical limbs that don't want to be removed), there are actually fewer cautions in the sequel than in the original. For a content breakdown, visit pluggedinonline.com.

Turn to Appendix II in the back of this book for thoughts about how superheroes tap into our yearning for the ultimate rescuer, Jesus Christ. Also worth reading is H. Michael Brewer's book *Who Needs a Superhero?: Finding Virtue, Vice, and What's Holy in the Comics.*

Just for Fun

Keep your eyes peeled when Peter and Norman are talking outside the science lab. Just after Peter mentions nanotechnology, the same red-haired girl in the purple sweater crosses right-to-left behind Norman in consecutive shots—an "extra" oops!

—Mick Silva

That Thing You Do!

Rated: PG
Themes: The sudden and fleeting nature of fame, following a dream, personality conflicts, pride, loyalty, the dark side of stardom, honoring a contract, respect in romantic love
Running Time: 1 hour, 45 minutes
Starring: Tom Everett Scott as Guy; Liv Tyler as Faye; Johnathon Schaech as Jimmy; Steve Zahn as Lenny; Tom Hanks as Mr. White; with Ethan Embry, Charlize Theron, and Giovanni Ribisi
Directed by: Tom Hanks

Cautions

A half-dozen profanities crop up. The worst is Lenny's use of "a—hole" (as he and Jimmy ask Guy to fill in for their wounded drummer). A deejay uses a crude term for a loss of virginity, though not in a sexual context. Also, the thrill of sudden fame yields enthusiastic cries of "oh my god!" There is some alcohol and tobacco use, and Lenny gambles in Vegas.

Story Summary

Remember when rock 'n' roll was musical sunshine? Breezy melodies. Contagious hooks. Innocent lyrics. Tom Hanks recaptures those days in *That Thing You Do!*, the funny, poignant tale of a fictional garage band from Erie, Pennsylvania that leaps from obscurity to national acclaim on the strength of one hit single in the summer of 1964. Likable young musicians struggle for recognition, achieve overnight success, learn that celebrity isn't all it's cracked up to be, and find the wild ride over as quickly as it began.

By day, Guy Patterson sells radios and clothes dryers for his controlling father at the family's appliance store. By night, he's a frustrated drummer who plays along with jazz records. When his friends lose their percussionist to a freak accident, they ask Guy to fill in so they can compete in a local talent show. Largely due to Guy speeding up their song's tempo, The Oneders (pronounced Wonders, though most people say O-nee-ders) win the contest and get a restaurant gig. Fans urge them to cut a demo. "That Thing You Do!" becomes a local sensation and attracts the attention of Play-Tone Records, which signs the boys to a contract, changes their name to The Wonders, and books them on a seasonal tour with other Play-Tone artists.

The diverse personalities in the band create an interesting dynamic. Lenny is a joker who drinks deeply from the cup of life with little concern that his beverage might be spiked. The affable Guy risks his father's ire by traveling with The Wonders, and proves to be the most stable, loyal member of the group. The nameless "bass player" exudes a childlike naïveté that's both an asset and a liability. As for the band's "leader," Jimmy is a brooding artist so deeply invested in his songwriting that he alienates his partners and ignores his most loyal fan, his sweet girlfriend, Faye.

Once on the Play-Tone label, the group's every move is choreographed by publicist Mr. White, a no-nonsense image specialist less concerned about art than marketing. Most of the boys are willing to jump through hoops. Not Jimmy. He resents being told what to do (lame interviews, silly photo ops, cameos in cheesy beach-party movies) and only wants to record more songs. After a blow-up with Faye and a meltdown in the studio, Jimmy quits, leaving what's left of the band in breach of contract. Not that anyone but Guy seems to care. Lenny has impulsively married a former Playboy bunny in Las Vegas, while the bass player is headed for the Marines. Mr. White tells Guy it's unlikely the label will sue:

Mr. White: It's a very common tale.

Guy: Well, maybe for you, but I was in a band and we still have a hit record.

Mr. White: Yeah, you do. One-hit Wonders. It's a very common tale.

Left alone in the studio, Guy lays down jazzy beats and recalls advice from his idol, Del Paxton: "There ain't no way to keep a band together. Bands come and go. You gotta keep on playin' no matter with who." Coincidentally, Del hears Guy playing and the pair jam a little. Not only does Guy get a professional break, he also makes a romantic connection with Faye. The film closes with humorous "where are they now" bios explaining how these fictional characters turned out. Written by, directed by, and co-starring Tom Hanks, *That Thing You Do!* is more than a two-time Oscar winner's vanity project; it's a retro treasure that gives families insight into the "business" part of show business.

Before You Watch

In the days prior to watching the film, find an excuse to take a drive together and listen to some pop music from the early to mid-1960s (your choice), as well as some more contemporary rock or R&B (let your teen choose). Without making value judgments, note differences in the melodies, tempo, lyrics, etc. and how they've changed over the years. As best you can, talk about what makes each style of music representative of its era and the cultural atmosphere that inspired it.

Bible Bookmarks

Rom. 12:15; Phil. 2:3-8; Acts 14:19-20; Eph. 6:4; 1 Cor. 13; Prov. 1:7, 4:23

Talking Points

1. Romans 12:15 says, "Rejoice with those who rejoice." Did you get a vicarious thrill seeing the band giddy with excitement over hearing their song on the radio? Share similar victories from your own lives.

151

2. What were some early signs that Jimmy wasn't a team player? Read Philippians 2:3-8 and Proverbs 1:7, and discuss our need for humility.

3. At the talent show, Jimmy couldn't enjoy the rabid applause because he was preoccupied with the fact that the song wasn't performed just the way he wrote it. The other guys went with the flow and had a blast. How can unfulfilled expectations rob us of joy if we're not willing to be flexible?

4. Which of The Wonders' perks (meeting famous people, travel, screaming fans, a film cameo, etc.) seemed most appealing to you? Why?

5. After a rough show, Guy's manager says, "You can't let a tepid reaction from one matinee house affect your dedication." What does he mean? How might this apply to Christ followers? Be inspired by the apostle Paul, who faced a tough crowd in Acts 14:19-20, but dusted himself off and went right back to work.

6. Guy's sour, sarcastic father lords over his store and his family. How does Ephesians 6:4 relate to his dad's words and behavior? How do you think Guy and his sister felt? If you're open to an honest answer, ask your teen if he or she has ever felt that way. When?

7. While working on the cheesy beach movie, Jimmy storms out, saying, "I guess I'm alone in my principles." Lenny jokes about it. When have you felt alone in your principles, and how did others react? Were those principles selfish or godly?

8. Contrast the ways Jimmy and Guy treated Faye. Which deserved her affection and why based on the definition of "love" in 1 Corinthians 13?

9. What does Faye mean when she says to Jimmy, "Shame on me for kissing you with my eyes closed so tight"? Read Proverbs 4:23. What can we learn from her mistake?

10. In life and in ministry God often partners us with personalities very different from our own. Those differences can enhance a group or tear it apart. That's true for a rock band, a family, a church group, a sports team, or just a handful of students assigned to work together on a class project. Ask, "What might you have done to try and preserve harmony in The Wonders?" "Is there a similar conflict needing attention in *your* life?" "What would be a healthy way of dealing with that challenge?" Be quick to listen, slow to offer advice, and prepared to pray.

Follow-Up Activity

The Wonders learned the hard way that even the most glamorous careers contain duties and pressures that aren't always fun. In 2004, a well-known TV and film actor called it quits, saying: "Here's how boring acting is: The longest that you get to do it, the *longest*, is about 90 seconds between 'action' and 'cut.' . . . Then, just as you're getting warmed up, it's, 'Cut, uh, we'll see you in about a half hour. We've got to move the camera around. Okay? Great. We'll see you in two hours.' And I can't do that any more."[11] Who would've guessed? If your teen has visions of a "dream job," do research together—not just to find out what skills or education are required, but to discover why it's called "work." Encourage your teen to interview people in the field. Ask about the job's downside. This isn't to discourage young people from chasing a dream, but to help them pursue it with both eyes wide open.

Just for Fun

The title song for the film was chosen as part of a contest held by 20th Century Fox. "That Thing You Do!" went on to earn an Oscar nomination for Best Original Song, and helped launch the career of songwriter Adam Schlesinger and his band Fountains of Wayne.

—*Bob Smithouser*

153

Tuck Everlasting

Rated: PG
Themes: Immortality, eternal youth, teen romance, releasing children, survivor's guilt, seizing the day, valuing stations of life, parental love
Running Time: 1 hour, 30 minutes
Starring: Alexis Bledel as Winnie Foster; Jonathan Jackson as Jesse Tuck; William Hurt as Angus; Sissy Spacek as Mae; with Ben Kingsley, Amy Irving, Scott Bairstow, and Victor Garber
Directed by: Jay Russell

Cautions

A man dies from a blow to the head. The film also includes images of people getting shot, torching a homestead, and falling from heights (no fatalities).

Story Summary

Set in 1914's Gilded Age of buckboards, general stores, and Edith Wharton, this story immediately introduces us to teens from two families that couldn't be more dissimilar. The only child of wealthy, controlling parents in a home ruled with snobbish propriety, Winnie Foster feels stifled, desperate to be liberated from her world of corsets and croquet. She's a caged songbird. By comparison, the scruffy, globe-trotting Tuck boys return home every decade or so to reconnect with Mom and Dad. Carefree rambling agrees with Jesse, though his older brother Miles seems consumed by brooding melancholy . . . and the burden of protecting a family secret.

When Winnie's parents announce plans to send her to a stuffy finishing

155

school, she flees the iron-gated confines of her family's estate into their nearby woods and happens upon Jesse drinking from a spring. Clearly, she has stumbled upon something she wasn't supposed to see. The nervous exchange between these strangers ends with Miles showing up, seizing Winnie, and carting her to their backwoods home. Night falls. Winnie's parents are desperate to find her. Meanwhile, a mysterious gentleman in a mustard-colored suit has been tracking the Tucks. He claims to be searching for long-lost relatives, though we sense his agenda may be more sinister.

At first a hostage of the reclusive yet hospitable Tucks, Winnie bonds with Jesse, who tenderly expands her horizons. Young love blossoms. Wanting to share these sweet moments forever, he decides to let her in on the big secret: *His family has discovered a spring of eternal life.* Not only has physical aging ceased, but those who drink its water are impervious to injury and death. Technically 104 years old, Jesse will be a spry 17 forever. And he wants Winnie to join him. Miles chimes in with the darker side of their immortality. He had a wife who refused to drink. She left him, convinced he'd made a pact with the devil, and wound up in an asylum. He also lost two young children, then fought in several wars, and saw thousands fall. He remains bitter.

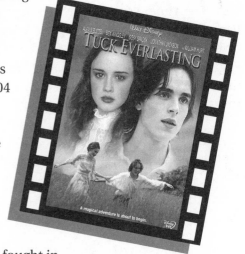

Angus, Jesse's dad, also hopes to dissuade Winnie from drinking. He explains, "One day you'll grow up. You'll do something important. You'll have children, maybe. And then one day you'll go out just like the flame of a candle [and] you'll make way for new life. That's a certainty. That's the natural way of things. Then there's us. What we Tucks have, you can't call it living. We just *are*. We're like rocks stuck at the side of a stream. . . . Don't be afraid of death, Winnie. Be afraid of the unlived life."

The man in the yellow suit locates Winnie and the Tucks, then agrees to lead the Fosters to their daughter in exchange for the property containing his secret prize. Just before the search party arrives, this dapper opportunist confronts the Tucks and, when Angus refuses to take him to the spring, threatens Winnie. Mae kills him with a blow from behind. Despite Winnie's plea on Mae's behalf, the boys' mother waits in jail to hang for murder until her sons mastermind her escape. The reunited family has no choice but to flee town, and as badly as Winnie wants to be with Jesse, she realizes joining them would invite a rabid search. Jesse tells her to drink from the spring, promising to come back for her when it's safe. The question is, *will she do it?* And would you? It's a provocative question at the center of a bittersweet film.

Before You Watch

Sit down with your teen and a stack of magazines that cover a range of interests, including fitness, fashion, and glamour. Page through them in search of articles or advertising that subtly preys on a desire to cling to youth. When you find an example share it and explain why you think it qualifies. Notice how rarely older models are used to sell products that aren't marketed directly to seniors. Why do think that is?

Bible Bookmarks

Rom. 8:15-17; Jn. 6:40; 1 Thess. 4:13-18; 1 Cor. 15:53-57; Isa. 46:3-4, 51:11; Ps. 92:14; Prov. 16:31; Rev. 21:4 and 6-7, 22:1-5; Phil. 1:23-24; 2 Cor. 5:1-5; Mk. 8:35-36

Talking Points

1. Ask your teen, "Can you relate to Winnie's restlessness?" As a parent, can you relate to her mother's desire to keep her a child forever? Explore that common tug-of-war as you saw it in the film and as it may be raging in your home. Why does holding onto some- one too tightly usually make him or her more desperate to break free?

2. Talk about the mysterious stranger's conversation with the cler- gyman in the cemetery, specifically how a confident Christian could be prepared to face death whenever "it is God's will" (Romans 8:15-17, John 6:40, 1 Thessalonians 4:13-18, 1 Corinthians 15:53-57).

3. What does Angus mean when he says, "You can't have livin'

without dyin"? Would our days on Earth be as precious if we had an unlimited supply? How does the brevity of life make time more meaningful?

4. Beyond a lust for more time, the man in the yellow suit wants to avoid "the stench and rot of old age." Is aging something to be feared? Why or why not? Does your culture respect the elderly or treat them as a burden? Get God's perspective on aging from Isaiah 46:3-4, Psalm 92:14, and Proverbs 16:31.

5. The amber-clad villain longs to drink from the spring *and* lord it over others by charging them for that privilege. Contrast this with God's attitude in Revelation 21:6-7.

6. Winnie discovers freedom in a world devoid of time where the pace is slower. Cavorting with Jesse is said to be "the first time Winnie felt free to explore, to ask questions, to play." Do you feel free to do these things? Why or why not? Would simplifying your world and slowing down help you enjoy life more?

7. What is a blessing to Jesse is a curse to Miles who argues, "Immortality ain't all the preachers crack it up to be." Read Philippians 1:23-24, 2 Corinthians 5:1-5, Isaiah 51:11, and Revelation 21:4 and 22:1-5. Note differences between the Tucks' earthbound immortality and the eternal life promised in Scripture.

8. How did you feel about Miles early in the movie? Did your opinion of him change? Why? What does this say about the need to extend grace to difficult people when we don't know the details of their story?

9. Angus asks Winnie, "Do you want to stay stuck as you are right now forever?" How would you answer that question? What would be the advantages? The drawbacks? Do you think Winnie made the right choice?

10. Jesse enjoys traversing the globe and collecting experiences with existential zeal, but there's a void without Winnie. Compare that "missing piece" to someone who drinks deeply from the cup of life but lacks a relationship with Jesus (Mark 8:35-36).

11. What do you think was going through Winnie's mind as she watched her mother cherish final moments with her grandmother? What did Angus mean when he advised, "Don't be afraid of death; be afraid of the unlived life"? Do you think these moments impacted her choice not to drink from the spring? Why?

Follow-Up Activity

If you and your teen have creative imaginations and enjoy filling in blanks, each of you could take a few days to invent the rest of Winnie's life story. What did she go on to do? Who did she marry? What were her children and grandchildren like? How did she interact with the many cultural changes that would arrive throughout the 20th century? Go out to dinner and compare notes. After sharing, make it a point to say that these are merely two of an infinite number of possibilities, and that just as many options await your teens as they proceed to seek God's will and write their own life stories.

Just for Fun

Did the young baseball player who taunts Winnie look familiar? The actor's name is Bradley Coryell, slightly older here than when he portrayed bully Big Boy Wilkinson in another *Movie Nights for Teens* pick, *My Dog Skip,* also directed by Jay Russell.

—Bob Smithouser

A Walk to Remember

Rated: PG
Themes: Redemption, peer pressure, trust, friendship, unconditional love, Christian faith, forgiveness, lifestyle evangelism, peace amid terminal illness, handling persecution, impact of divorce on teens
Running Time: 1 hour, 42 minutes
Starring: Mandy Moore as Jamie Sullivan; Shane West as Landon Carter; Peter Coyote as Reverend Sullivan; Daryl Hannah as Cynthia Carter
Directed by: Adam Shankman

Cautions

The movie's main problem is teen profanity (about two dozen instances, half of them s-words). There's also some randy joking, implied underage drinking, and a secret handshake that mimics dragging on a marijuana cigarette. While disappointing, this serves to contrast Landon's and Jamie's worlds. He's a *real* bad-boy in need of *real* redemption. And her light shines all the brighter against this shadowy backdrop of teen life. Even so, some families may want to look for the "edited-for-TV" version. (The heaviest dose of inappropriate behavior is in the opening scene.)

Story Summary

A Walk to Remember is based on a popular work of teen fiction by Nicholas Sparks. Although it's not a Christian film, it's a powerful tale of one young believer's ability to influence the lives of those in her small, coastal North Carolina town, including an unruly young rebel.

Jamie Sullivan isn't "cool." She's quiet, studious, and wears unfashionably modest clothes that would embarrass most girls. But not Jamie. She isn't a slave to style and doesn't care what other people think. Her self-confidence comes from how God sees her and who she is on the inside. She's witty, self-assured, wise, and caring, though few of her peers get close enough to notice. All they see is the bland, goody-two-shoes daughter of the local preacher.

At the other end of the spectrum lies Landon Carter, a brooding member of the in crowd who is sassy, angry, self-absorbed, and occasionally cruel. His aimless clique enjoys teasing Jamie. Their worlds collide when Landon is punished after a thoughtless prank lands a boy in the hospital. His sentence includes tutoring disadvantaged students on weekends and acting in the school play—activities he'd never do voluntarily. Coincidentally, Jamie is already involved in both.

Landon observes her decency in action, but responds with sarcasm and ridicule. Jamie continues to be kind to him in spite of his rudeness, helping him learn his lines for the show. But she's no doormat. She puts him in his place with sharp insight and sly wit. Consequently, something about her quiet strength and self-respect attracts him. He wants to be around her, but knows it could cost him popularity points if his pals learn how he really feels. Months later, while acting opposite Jamie in the spring musical, Landon is so overcome with emotion that he forgets his lines and adds an unscripted kiss.

Landon sincerely reaches out to Jamie. She doesn't trust him at first. In the spirit of Jeremiah 13:23, she wonders if this leopard can change his spots. So Landon sets out to prove himself. He gives her a new sweater, then defends her honor when his jealous ex-girlfriend plays a malicious joke. Undeterred by her father's "no dating" rule, he respectfully asks her dad for permission to take her out. Landon's bad-boy reputation isn't an easy thing for the pious, protective Reverend Sullivan to overlook, but he believes in forgiveness and trusts his daughter's

162

instincts. Soon Landon is helping Jamie complete items on a "to-do list" she has developed for her life.

As the relationship deepens and sweetens, Landon changes, adapting to what's important to Jamie. Then one evening Jamie confesses that she has leukemia and isn't responding to treatments. Landon races to the home of his estranged father, a physician, in hopes that he might have a solution. But no one can help. It's just a matter of time. Landon's only choice is to marry her and spend whatever time they have left making her as happy as possible. It's merely a summer, though he recalls it was perfect with "more love than lots of people know in a lifetime. And then she went, with her unfailing faith."

Four years later, Landon visits Jamie's father to drop off a memento and tell him he's headed to medical school. His path has changed because of Jamie's living witness and her love. Landon reminisces, "Jamie saved my life. She taught me everything about life, hope, and the long journey ahead." We're not sure that he ever adopted her faith, but it's clear he has been changed forever by a life well lived.

Before You Watch

Sometime prior to your Movie Night, casually initiate a discussion about typical Hollywood portrayals of Christianity. How are "religious" people depicted? Be specific. You may even want to make a game of it, going back and forth summoning characters and scenes you've encountered. The more examples you recall, the more likely you'll notice a negative trend. After watching *A Walk to Remember*, refer back to this conversation and decide how this film measures up.

Bible Bookmarks

1 Cor. 13 and 6:18; Matt. 18:21-22; 2 Cor. 6:13-15; Prov. 29:18; 1 Thess. 4:7; 1 Pet. 1:15; Mk. 9:35, 11:25; Jer. 13:23, 29:11; Hab. 1:5; Eph. 4:31-32

Talking Points:

1. Peer pressure and the desire to be accepted caused Clay Gephart to do something foolish. Why is that temptation so

163

strong? (Talk about how Christ's unconditional love can satisfy that need.) How can we know when a "harmless prank" crosses the line?

2. On the bus, Jamie tells Landon, "Please don't pretend you know me, okay?" What does it take to truly know someone and be a friend? What qualities attract you to your closest friends?

3. Proverbs 29:18 says, "Where there is no vision, the people perish." Compare Jamie's specific list of ambitions to the aimlessness of Landon and his crew. How can a lack of vision—spiritual or otherwise—put us on a road to nowhere?

4. Landon starts to change when he stops being selfish and focuses on others' needs. Why do you think that happens? In what ways are *you* fulfilling Mark 9:35 by serving others?

5. The pastor is angry with his daughter for giving Landon a quick goodnight kiss. How do you feel about certain displays of affection before marriage? In an attempt to honor 1 Corinthians 6:18, what boundaries have you and your family set for dating? What kinds of situations can be dangerous to purity?

6. Jamie tells her father she thinks God wants her "to be happy." Surely God doesn't want us to be miserable, but how could Jamie's assumption lead a Christian into trouble? Talk about the need to subjugate *happiness* to *holiness* (1 Thessalonians 4:7, 1 Peter 1:15).

7. Many teens engage in "missionary dating" in hopes of converting an unsaved person who has caught their eye. Why is that a bad idea? What does 2 Corinthians 6:13-15 say about dating someone who's not a believer? Under the circumstances, should Jamie and Landon have gotten involved? Married? Why or why not?

8. In Jamie's hospital room, Landon reads from 1 Corinthians 13. Read that passage and identify ways each showed that kind of love to the other.

9. If you've already watched *Finding Neverland,* compare the way characters in each film coped with terminal illness. How did Jamie's faith in God differ from the hope manufactured by J. M. Barrie for his dying friend?

10. Jamie makes these two statements: "I do not need a reason to be angry with God" and "Maybe God has a bigger plan for me than I had for myself." What do you think occurred in her heart *between* those comments? Can you relate to her frustration? Her peace? Read Jeremiah

29:11 and Habakkuk 1:5 for a reminder that God has big plans for His children.

11. How do you think Landon's strained relationship with his father impacted his rebelliousness? Discuss Landon's ability to forgive his Dad, and how several of the boy's old friends sought his forgiveness (a virtue explored in Mark 11:25, Matthew 18:21-22, and Ephesians 4:31-32). Do you need to forgive someone who has hurt you? Do you need to ask someone for forgiveness?

Follow-Up Activity

Each of you make your own "life to-do" lists. Include serious goals, fun aspirations, and even some outrageous dreams. Plan a follow-up outing, just you and your teen, and share your desires with each other. As a parent, think of ways you might be able to help make some of your teen's dreams a reality.

If your family likes to build things, try making a telescope together like Landon did. Books are available at your local library. Or conduct an online search for "make your own telescope," which should turn up several Web sites offering projects of varying difficulties.

Just for Fun

The first time we see Jamie she's walking toward Landon and his friends in front of the school, carrying a box, and wearing a backpack. But as the camera swings behind her to show her walking away, the backpack has mysteriously disappeared. Oops!

—*Lissa Halls Johnson*

165

Appendix I: Life Lessons from Middle-earth

Following the release of the *Lord of the Rings* movies, I asked members of the cast this question: "While working on these films, did you learn a life lesson that would be valuable for teenagers today?" Consider using each response as a spark plug for family dialogue.

Viggo Mortensen (Aragorn): "The lesson, I guess, is that the union with others is more significant than your individual existence. It doesn't deny the importance of your individuality. It just means you're a better person the more you connect with others. You're going to know more. You're going to be stronger and you're going to have a better life if you get over yourself. That's part of growing up. . . . There's the one side that is 'get over yourself, listen to others, and don't be selfish,' but you have to balance that with 'think for yourself and don't believe everything you hear.' We all have to do that."

Sean Astin (Sam): "Contentment. That you can't do everything all at once, right away. Be patient and take things as they come. Learn to live each moment. It's the age-old thing that any 25- to 35-year-old person tries to tell a 15- to 20-year-old, but that they're destined not to learn until they're 25. As a 31-year-old man, I've finally gotten to that place."

Miranda Otto (Eowyn): "*Lord of the Rings* reveres and talks about things I think society is aching to go back to. A lot of films these days concentrate on so many negative aspects of society. In the '40s, [onscreen] ideals were about honor, loyalty, and dignity—qualities that we tend to forego so quickly for money. If someone says, 'I'll give you two hundred dollars if you take your clothes off and run around the block,' a lot of people will do it."

Peter Jackson (director): "The need for determination. You have to believe in yourself and not let anything stand in your way. There have been several periods in the history of this project when it could've just died. People refer to luck and say it was lucky that New Line wanted to do a movie when Miramax turned it down, and it was lucky they wanted to do three movies instead of two and all this. I don't actually believe in luck. I think you sort of create your own luck."

Andy Serkis (Gollum): "Not seeing someone and taking them at face value. You can't help but sense what's going on in the world around you when you're making these films. Obviously we started before 9/11, and these things have been in the back of my mind. The threat of war. The inability to see another person's point of view. I feel it's important to understand the nature of the dark and light sides of our personalities."

Ian McKellen (Gandalf): "My parents brought me up to think that one had a 'prime of life' and that it wasn't going to happen anytime soon. You had to wait. You had to earn your prime when you knew what life was about and you were accomplishing something. And then the Beatles came along and told us that the best time of your life was when you were young, and I thought I'd rather missed out. But here I am at 64 and this is my prime of life. That would be my message: Don't worry. Don't try and hit it too early because your time might be later on. I think everyone has a different prime of life. Mine just happened rather late."

Brad Dourif (Grima Wormtongue): "The whole theme of fear and confrontation with yourself. Either we confront our fear or we don't, and what happens if you don't is really pathetic. What you're afraid of seems bigger than you are, but if you let it overwhelm you and overcome you it makes you small. If you face it, you triumph and become much more."

John Rhys-Davies (Gimli and the voice of Treebeard): "Unity, courage, and a willingness to sacrifice yourself. We need the spirituality of the elf; the earthy, indestructible qualities of the dwarf; and above all the good, simple hearts of the hobbits. And we must aspire to be the king that has yet to come into his place. We all have a choice; we are either slaves or we are princes. We make slaves of ourselves so readily and so easily."

Dominic Monaghan (Merry): "If you keep what's pure—love of friends, your family, or defending something good and honest that you believe in—as opposed to greed, power, hunger, and domination, then it seems to ring true that you'll have the best kind of fate. That's what the hobbits stand for."

Billy Boyd (Pippin): "Don't get all stressed out wondering where your next 10 years are going to go. Partly from playing a hobbit and partly from living in New Zealand, which has a more laid-back lifestyle, I've learned to be more happy in what's happening now."

Liv Tyler (Arwen): "I learned about patience and trust more than anything, because it was such a long experience. Obviously we had all of this great material and we were quite clear, yet we also weren't a lot of times. We'd shoot a scene and a couple months later they would completely change it and shoot a scene with other characters and give them those same words. There's so much in the movie that would happen like that. So I learned to be patient and trust Peter [Jackson] to use the best material and do what was right. It's hard to trust somebody that much. I think that can be relevant in school with a teacher. You sort of think you have all the answers. I felt on this movie there were a couple times I made mistakes and I wish I had listened more to Peter. It has definitely made me more aware of that."

169

Karl Urban (Eomer): "How Viggo [Mortensen] threw himself into his work was an inspiration to the younger cast members. He stood in the rain and sleet for three solid months of night shoots with no complaint. Then he chips a tooth in the middle of a fight and wants to superglue it back in and keep fighting so he doesn't hold up production."

Bernard Hill (King Theoden): "That it's only prosthetic deep. Let me explain. For the battle scenes we learned sword positions and practiced a lot. Because it can be dangerous, we needed to learn to trust each other. So we'd hang out with the stunt guys in trousers and such and really got to know each other. When it came time for filming the Helm's Deep scenes, they'd arrive in makeup and Uruk-hai armor with their false teeth in and we'd hear the call, 'Okay, heads on!' So they'd put their heads on and come at us and you couldn't tell who was who. My immediate reaction was, 'Ugh, I don't like this person.' Then you'd hear 'Hey, Shaw!' 'Who's that?' 'Andy.' 'Oh Andy, hi!' Inside this head was my friend. But with the head on something happened to him. I was frightened of this person because of an appearance that was only prosthetic deep. It forced me to think about my fears and innate prejudice."

Elijah Wood (Frodo): "You don't realize how important your friends are until you need them. . . . During tough times when you lose perspective or have mental or emotional fatigue, those are the people who pick you up and tell you, 'It's cool. We're in this together.' Embrace those friends that you have."

Orlando Bloom (Legolas): "I think friendship and the fellowship of strangers, mixed races putting aside their differences to come together and make a difference. Legolas and Gimli couldn't be further apart and yet they kind of, you know [he quotes from the film], 'What about standing side by side with a friend?' There's something about having the wisdom, courage, and compassion to live life with integrity. All of the characters within *The Lord of the Rings* act with integrity. So I think the message to the kids is courage, humility, and integrity."

Appendix II: Why We Love Superheroes

Have you ever wondered why we find certain superheroes so appealing? Take Spider-Man for instance. You start with Peter Parker, a normal guy who snaps pictures for the school paper. He sees the world much like we do, albeit through a camera lens. Suddenly the mother of all spider bites sends him climbing the walls battling evil. Oh, he's still Peter Parker. He eats, sleeps, and puts on his red-and-blue jumpsuit one leg at a time just like the rest of us. But he's *special*.

Or how about Superman? While not a native of earth (he was sent here as a baby from another galaxy), he's mortal, speaks perfect English, and looks like a *GQ* cover boy. Yet mild-mannered Clark Kent also possesses amazing strength, plus the ability to fly and see through things. Like Spidey, Mr. Incredible, Hulk, Flash, the X-Men, and countless other beloved characters, he is simultaneously human and superhuman—a person who can intimately relate to mankind, yet is uniquely empowered to save humanity from its current malaise.

Sound like anyone you know?

I believe we are wired by our Creator to resonate with that kind of hero. Jesus Christ arrived on this cosmic dirt clod as a baby, fully divine, yet fully man (Philippians 2:5-11). He got hungry, thirsty, and tired just as we do. He was a blue-collar laborer. He laughed, loved, and cried. He knew betrayal and pain. Hebrews 5:15 says, "For we do not have a high priest who is unable to sympathize with our weaknesses, but we have one who has been tempted in every way, just as we are—yet without sin."

At the appointed time, Jesus shed his secret identity—a carpenter whose time had "not yet come" (John 2:4)—and began working miracles, displaying amazing spiritual strength and yes, even seeing through things (including a Samaritan woman in John 4:16-19). He came to rescue us. Not by soaring through town in a flashy red cape, but by humbly enlisting us into His own heavenly Justice League before heroically laying down His life. He is the one uniquely empowered to save humanity from its *eternal* malaise.

Throughout history, cultures have concocted second-rate saviors that tap into people's inherent need for a man-god. The most popular

173

hero in Greek mythology was Hercules, sired by Zeus and born of a mortal woman. Destined to be the lord of his people, Hercules looked, walked, and talked like your rank-and-file Athenian, yet he exhibited extraordinary strength and went on to rule as an immortal god on Mount Olympus. Or so the story goes.

The parallels between fact and fiction don't stop with the good guys. Nearly every superhero must contend with a supervillain, usually a disgruntled megalomaniac bent on ruling or destroying mankind. Just as Spider-Man battles the Green Goblin high above the city streets, the Lord and his angels war against forces of darkness on our behalf in heavenly realms. There has never been a more ambitious, frustrated, or vengeful supervillain than Satan, the scheming, lying adversary of Jesus who himself wears disguises to conceal his true identity (2 Corinthians 11:13-15). Just as we shouldn't lose sight of Christ's ultimate heroism, it would be equally unwise to underestimate the real supervillain currently at large.

I'm not suggesting that Spider-Man and his comic book peers are dangerous counterfeits out to distract us from the One who truly deserves our affection. We simply need to connect the dots back to Jesus. After all, He's the genuine article! Hollywood has handed us a golden opportunity. Let's capitalize on it by helping others see how modern heroes can unintentionally point to mankind's inner longing for the real Savior.

—*Bob Smithouser*

Appendix III: A Biblical Case for Discernment

Does God care which movies we watch? Absolutely! While the Bible may not mention Hollywood by name, it gives us plenty of principles that apply to entertainment. How are we wired? What type of content is healthy? What should we avoid? And how can we build a defense that lets us work through the "gray areas" armed with biblical truth? The following mini-concordance will help you guide your teen through verses critical to a deeper understanding of media discernment:

The War Within Us

John 3:1-21	• Jesus talks about flesh and spirit
Ephesians 2:1-5	• The sinful nature brings death
Ephesians 4:17-24	• Out with the old, in with the new
Romans 7:14-25	• Paul admits his own struggles
Romans 8:1-17	• Jesus: Cure for the sinful nature
Galatians 5:16-25	• Keys to living by the Spirit

Avoiding Indecent Exposure

Psalm 11:4-7	• The dangers of loving violence
Psalm 101	• David's pledge of purity
Philippians 4:4-8	• Your heart's best defense
1 Thessalonians 5:21-22	• Test everything
Colossians 2:8	• Watch out for deceivers!
Colossians 3:1-10	• Trading junk for jewels
1 Timothy 4:7-16	• A call to young Christians
2 Timothy 4:3-4	• Don't waffle on the truth
Exodus 20:1-21	• God's original Top-10 list

Preparing a Defense

Ephesians 6:10-18	• The full armor of God
Matthew 6:19-24	• Protecting the eyes
Proverbs 4:23-27	• Guard your heart
1 Peter 1:13-16	• Follow the Commander
2 Peter 1:3-11	• Weapons of spiritual battle

Psalm 119:9-16	• Armed with God's resources
1 Corinthians 9:24-27	• Training to win
2 Corinthians 10:3-5	• Taking thoughts prisoner
Romans 12:1-2	• Don't be *con*formed; be *trans*formed
1 Thessalonians 4:3-8	• Control your passions

The Value of Wisdom

1 Kings 3:7-12	• Solomon asks for discernment
Proverbs 3:21-26	• Benefits of discernment
Genesis 41:15-40	• Joseph interprets dreams
Ecclesiastes 9:13-18	• A tale of wisdom as strength
Matthew 5:10-16	• Salt and light to the world
John 10:1-18	• Knowing the Shepherd's voice
Philippians 1:9-11	• The apostles' prayer for you

Notes

Introduction
1. "Do Movies Matter?—Part 2," *Entertainment Weekly*, November 28, 2003.
2. *USA Today*, June 23, 2003.
3. Associated Press, February 18, 2003.
4. *USA Today*, January 22, 2003.
5. *Time*, January 31, 2005.
6. From the speech, "History and Politics on the Screen," delivered to the Center for Popular Culture, February 24, 1996.
7. *Interview*, November 1994.
8. *Interview*, February 1999.
9. *Rolling Stone*, October 30, 2003.
10. *Time*, August 16, 2004.
11. *Basic Christianity*, John R. W. Stott, InterVarsity Press, London, 1971.
12. "Do You Know Where Your Children Are?" by Liza Mundy, *Washington Post*, November 16, 2003.
13. "Movie Ratings Losing Value?" by Ed Vitagliano, *AgapePress*, October 20, 2004.

The Movies
1. "Apocalypse Soon? No, But This Movie (and Democrats) Hope You'll Think So" by Patrick J. Michaels, *The Washington Post*, May 16, 2004.
2. *USA Today*, May 4, 2004.
3. Notes by Ronald Blythe in the 1966 reprint of the novel *Emma* by Jane Austen, the Penguin English Library.
4. *Chicago Sun-Times*, September 13, 1996.
5. *Time*, October 25, 2004.
6. Press notes for *The Incredibles*, distributed by Walt Disney Pictures.
7. As described in Tolkien's supplementary work *The Silmarillion*.

8. *Entertainment Weekly,* August 22/29, 2003.
9. Press Notes for *Signs,* Touchstone Pictures, 2002.
10. *Entertainment Weekly,* 2004 Fall Movie Preview issue.
11. E! Online, "Corbett Gives Two Films' Notice," Sept. 28, 2004, by Larry Carroll.

About the Author

Bob Smithouser is editor of *Plugged In* magazine, Focus on the Family's award-winning parents' guide to entertainment and popular youth culture. He also reviews films for "Life on the Edge Live" and pluggedin online.com. A husband and father of two, Bob has spent more than a decade monitoring the culture, answering teens' media questions, and teaching biblical discernment to families. He holds an M.A. in Communications from the University of Kentucky.

About the Contributing Writers

Brandy Bruce is an assistant editor in Focus on the Family's book publishing department. She lives in Castle Rock, Colorado, with her husband, Jeff, and their cat, Georgia.

Lissa Halls Johnson is a book producer, writer, and fiction acquisitions editor for Focus on the Family. She is the creator and editor of the "Brio Girls" book series. She has written 15 novels for teenagers and young readers.

Mick Silva graduated from Westmont College in 1996 and married his junior high sweetheart in 2000. As the dad of a two-year-old daughter, he is a highly distracted editor in Focus on the Family's book publishing department.

FOCUS ON
yourchild®
FROM FOCUS ON THE FAMILY®

Dear Friend,

Being a dad is a great privilege. It's been the most exciting, overwhelming, and unforgettable experience that's ever happened to me! If you've also had the privilege of parenting, I'm sure you feel the same way.

But I know another feeling most of us moms and dads have: "Who can I turn to that understands what I'm dealing with?"

That's why Focus on Your Child was launched by Focus on the Family. We're here to help you find answers and enjoy the journey of raising your kids. It's never been easier to find the help and encouragement you've been looking for.

I invite you to visit our Web site at **www.focusonyourchild.com** and see for yourself just how much great parenting insight is waiting there for you to explore. And while you're there, you can sign up for a complimentary membership that includes many "parenting perks," including audio journals and newsletters based on the ages of your children.

Parenting is an adventure — let us help you enjoy the journey!

Sincerely,

Leon Lowman Jr.
Senior Director, Focus on Your Child

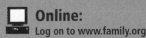

Use Mainstream Movies to Teach Truth

Movie Nights for Kids
Movie Nights for Kids highlights 25 fun, interesting films such as *Spy Kids* and *Tarzan* that parents can use to teach powerful lessons to children. Each selection includes engaging activities, a plot summary, and discussion points that strengthen a Christian worldview. This essential guide shows parents how to use contemporary movies to teach eternal truths to their children in a fun, easy way. Paperback.

Also available, **Movie Nights: 25 Movies to Spark Spiritual Discussions with Your Teen.** Paperback.

Fuel: 10 Minute Devotions to Ignite the Faith of Parents and Teens
Fuel helps busy teens connect with their parents. Youth expert Joe White has put together powerful 10-minute devotions from the New Testament for you to share. It's fun, fast and filled with memorable stories, discussion starters, and lifeline applications all designed to get parents and teens talking. Paperback.

Lead Your Teen to a Lifelong Faith– A Workbook For Parents
Quit clutching and start coaching! Walking alongside your teen, you can help him build a faith that survives the turbulent waters ahead. *Lead Your Teen to a Lifelong Faith* is perfect for individuals or groups. You'll find practical insights, Scripture, humor, and even a leader's guide. Ignite your teen's passion for following Christ! Paperback.

● ● ●

Look for these special books in your Christian bookstore or request a copy by calling (800) A-FAMILY (232-6459). Friends in Canada may write Focus on the Family, PO Box 9800, Stn Terminal, Vancouver, BC V6B 4G3 or call (800) 661-9800.

Visit our Web site (www.family.org) to learn more about the ministry or find out if there is a Focus on the Family office in your country.